D0989854

BRITISH LORRIES
OF THE
40s and 50s

First published in 1989 by Roundoak Publishing,
(an imprint of Nynehead Books) Nynehead,
Wellington, Somerset, England, TA21 OBX.

Copyright © 1989 Peter Davies & Roundoak
Publishing

All rights reserved. No part of this publication may be
reproduced (except for the purposes of review), stored
in a retrieval system, or transmitted in any form or by
any means, electronic, mechanical, optical, photo-
copying, recording or otherwise without prior written
permission of the publisher.

British Library Cataloguing in Publication Data

Davies, Peter

  1. Trucks–Great Britain–History
  I. Title
  629.2'24

ISBN 1-871565-01-4

Designed by Peter Davies

Jacket photograph:
In the setting of Liverpool Docks, this 1953 ERF 5.6TS 'chinese six'
flat, with its bagged load, roundly sums up the flavour of road
haulage in the early post-war years, when drivers grafted by the sweat
of their brow loading up in dusty Victorian mills.

End Papers:
This interesting shot taken at Dunstable in 1959 depicts an assort-
ment of BRS eight wheelers mirrored in the mill-pond surface of the
water-logged yard. The clarity of the reflected image is highlighted in
the rear endpapers where by 'photographic trickery' the picture has
been inverted. The vehicles shown are, left to right, a 1954 ERF 6.8, a
1953 AEC Mk III Mammoth Major, and two Bristol HG6Ls from 1957
& 1952.

Printed in Great Britain by the Amadeus Press,
Huddersfield, West Yorkshire

BRITISH LORRIES
OF THE
40s and 50s

Peter Davies

Roundoak Publishing, Nynehead, Wellington, Somerset

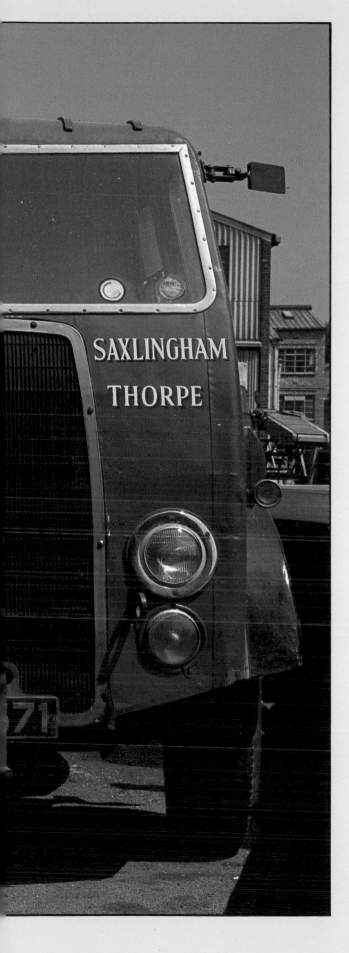

Contents

Left: Sentinel diesels, perhaps the most handsome of all British lorries, pose for the camera at a Norfolk flour mill.

Shades of life in the fifties, a Thames Trader overtakes a BRS
Leyland Octopus on the Great North Road. Meanwhile an AA
patrolman renders assistance to a motorist in trouble.

Preface

How often do you hear the phrase, "If only I could turn the clock back"?
It is only human to indulge in memories of bygone days. Obviously
it is not possible to literally re-live the past, but thankfully media
exist by which we can at least conjure up reminders of yesteryear.

Living artefacts provide us with a direct link to times past, and,
by preserving cherished objects, we can perpetuate experiences which
would otherwise be lost. As the march of progress goes on, some of
these objects become little more than curiosities.

Photography provides us with a means of preserving images –
scenes which might only exist for a fleeting instant
can be frozen in time and enjoyed for posterity.

Countless images might exist in the mind's eye,
often blurred by fading memories,
but once an image is recorded on film, especially in full colour,
it can serve as a lasting reminder for all to share.

So it is that photography has become a means to an end for me –
not as a hobby in itself, but to enable me to capture
precious images of road transport.

When I first began to photograph lorries in the mid fifties, it was
with a crude camera with black and white film.
Consequently many of my early pictures are lacking in technical quality.
Some of these have been reproduced in this book, where subjects are of
interest. Later photographs, especially those in colour, are of better quality.

Whatever the quality – I hope the following pages will provide you with
a journey down the memory lanes of road transport.

Journey Back...

Bomb scarred cities, food rationing, fuel shortages – on the face of it the early post war years seem to present few reasons for nostalgia. Nevertheless the forties and fifties hold special memories for many, not least for those involved in road haulage. The nation was shrouded in austerity, and until commercial vehicle manufacturers got back on their feet after the war, most transport firms were unable to obtain new vehicles. Work-worn lorries from the thirties could be seen struggling on with smoky exhausts, balding tyres and with one headlight masked off from the 'blackout' era. Yet curiously enough the hardship and pioneering spirit of the period heightens the feeling of nostalgia.

Transport operators had gone through tough times under tight government controls during the war years. Fuel and tyre shortages had led to restrictions on vehicle usage but because of its inherent flexibility, road transport was still called upon to maintain vital supplies. Efforts on the part of the government to force a greater proportion of traffic on to the railways and even the waterways, only served to highlight the superior efficiency of road transport.

Having been denied the freedom to run their lorries as they knew best, hauliers who hoped for a peacetime return to free enterprise promptly found themselves under more state control. The Ministry of War Transport 'Road Transport Organisation' which was the wartime body set up in 1942 to direct transport operations nationally was kept in being for more than a year by the Labour Government elected in 1945. In effect it was a foretaste of the nationalisation announced by that government in the 1946 Transport Bill against fierce opposition from the haulage industry.

The Road Haulage Association mounted a concerted anti-nationalisation campaign which, in spite of widespread support at all levels, was to no avail. The 1947 Transport Act called for all long distance road transport (over 40 miles radius, later reduced to 25 miles) to be brought under the control of a newly formed British Transport Commission. Under the terms of the Act a Road Transport Executive (later the

The driver's greatcoat was a must for winter warmth. Headlamp masks, white painted wings and the absence of chromed or polished alloy fittings mark this clearly as a war-time scene. The year is 1944. (Photo: Maudslay Motor Co.)

Road Haulage Executive) was empowered to acquire all firms who were engaged in long distance road haulage and to control them from eight divisional headquarters set up nationally.

'Own-account' or 'C-licence' operators were exempted and certain other traffics notably meat transport, furniture removals, heavy haulage and bulk liquid transport were to be handled by special departments also within the general control of the BTC. General haulage and parcels operations came under British Road Services.

The process of buying thousands of companies into state control was long, complicated and, to many of the operators, traumatic. Many long established hauliers who had built up successful operations over two or three decades did not take kindly to this apparent invasion by the state. Some even refused point blank to co-operate, locking their vehicles away and conveniently 'losing' the keys. On the other hand many firms, in particular those in a poor financial state and struggling for business, were more than happy to hand over the reins.

So long and drawn out was the procedure for acquiring the 4000 or so companies subject to nationalisation that it was never fully implemented. At the general election of 1951 the Conservatives were returned to power and with their commitment to free enterprise set about dismantling the cumbersome monolith of nationalisation.

Following the Transport Act 1953, the Road Haulage Disposal Board was set up to sell off the vehicles and premises back into private hands whilst the BRS retained fleet was left to operate on a basis of fair competition with the free enterprise haulage companies. The disposals were spread over a three year period up to 1956. The much reduced BRS organisation, now BRS Limited, operated under the BTC until 1963 when this was finally wound up and the Transport Holding Company was formed.

Strong though the anti-nationalisation feeling was amongst hauliers in the late forties and early fifties, BRS did win the devoted attention of one section of the community. It gave rise to a great deal of interest among transport enthusiasts, who were happily distanced from the political turmoil. Without question a whole cult grew up around the plain red lorries which could be seen the length and breadth of the country. It became a hobby on a similar scale to train spotting and drew together a band of enthusiasts who have dedicated themselves to the study of haulage ever since.

While a large proportion of lorries of the period appeared in the unmistakable 'Ayres Red' livery, there were still hundreds of other colour schemes around to add variety. Own-account vehicles still carried the brand names of famous manufacturers. There was indeed an upsurge in C-licence operators, coinciding with the formation of BRS. Many large manufacturers who had regular transport requirements, involving

distribution of finished products and movement of raw materials, chose to run their own fleets. Some acquired haulage companies who wanted to escape state control and ran them as subsidiaries. This would not have been possible had it not been for last minute changes in the Transport Bill which exempted own-account operators from inclusion in BRS.

Though in Kellogg's livery this 1951 Guy Vixen was one of a fleet operated by BRS Contracts. (Photo: Ted Oates Collection)

Many C-licence operators preferred to keep transport under their own control as it often called for specialist knowledge and experience with vehicles tailored to their specific needs. While many of the C-licence vehicles were employed on local journeys some of the larger fleets were employed on long distance routes taking manufactured goods to customers and distribution centres and returning with raw materials for the owner's business. Very often though, what first appeared to be a C-licence vehicle turned out to be a BRS lorry operating under contract.

Many of the larger fleets acquired in the process of nationalisation served established contract customers and BRS continued to operate those contracts.

Haulage companies whose operations were mainly confined to short and medium distance work were exempted from nationalisation but their journeys were limited to a radius of 25 miles from base.

Special traffics which included bulk liquids, furniture removals and heavy haulage were handled by other departments of the BTC under the 'Pickfords' banner. Pickfords became part of the BTC automatically as it belonged to the mainline railway companies and was nationalised along with them in 1948. The railway companies had acquired large transport interests, which included Pickfords and Carter Paterson, as far back as 1933. In fact both these companies had had a long working relationship with the Railways, going back to the mid-19th century.

If there is one issue which has seemed to unite politicians from both sides over the the decades it is the determination to prop up the railways' share of freight. In spite of this, road haulage, without which the railways could not function, has progressively gained a bigger and bigger share of freight traffic.

The 1933 Road & Rail Traffic Act imposed strict licensing on road haulage, coming into effect from 1st April 1934. Directly or indirectly this was meant to curb expansion and to move more goods on to the railways.

Nationalisation was itself intended to achieve greater co-ordination between road and rail.

So, the Road Haulage Executive found itself in control of the vast Pickfords organisation which was not, strictly speaking, in long distance general haulage, and therefore would not have been subject to nationalisation. It was to form the Special Traffics Division, a separate organisation within the BTC.

Pickfords operations were diverse, covering household removals on one end of the scale, and the movement of abnormal indivisible loads on the other. In

The Tank Haulage division of Pickfords operated a wide variety of types. A typical medium weight artic is seen here in the form of a petrol engined Bedford 'SA' dating from 1951. It has a Scammell automatic coupling and 1400 gallon tank by Thompson of Bilston. (Photo: Vauxhall Motors Ltd)

between, and nearest to normal long distance type operation, was the Tank Haulage Division with depots in London, Liverpool, Bromborough, Manchester and Hull. They ran a mixed fleet, including many maximum weight rigid eight wheelers, mainly of AEC, Atkinson and Albion manufacture. A large number of these did not appear in the standard Pickfords livery of dark blue, but carried the names of contract customers including well known petrol and chemical companies.

On the heavy haulage operation Pickfords had 25 depots strategically located in areas of heavy industry.

The household removals fleet was also nationally based with around 200 branches and the familiar Guy 'Vixen' and Bedford 'O-type' pantechnicons were a common sight in every town and city.

Apart from the addition of the BTC 'lion and wheel' badge on the door, Pickfords vehicles retained their pre-war dark blue livery with white signwriting and red

wheels throughout the fifties. A new livery in lighter blue and orange appeared in 1972.

Another common sight in the fifties were the lorries of BRS Meat Cartage Division. This department was based on the former Hay's Wharf organisation and at its height had 15 depots among which were London (Smithfield Market and Poplar), Liverpool, Bootle, Bristol, Southampton, Glasgow, Manchester and Newcastle-on-Tyne. The vehicles were used to transport meat in insulated containers, mainly from dock to market. Operations were at their busiest in the late forties and early fifties when rationing was in force and home production could not match demand. As home supplies improved and imports declined so the meat haulage operation diminished. From 1956 the operations came under BRS (Meat Haulage) Ltd. The familiar dark blue drawbar tractors with pale cream coloured demountable containers on 4-wheeled trailers could be seen well into the sixties but were eventually swallowed up into the Union Cartage Company. On long distance work, BRS (Meat Haulage) Ltd used

Typical BRS Meat Haulage tractor and trailer outfit seen manoeuvring in London's busy Smithfield Market. The tractor is an Austin 'Series 3' for up to 15 tons GTW.

TUM 361, a 1954 ERF in the BRS 'Ayres' red livery stands alongside ULD 675, a 1957 Leyland Beaver and trailer in the dark blue and cream of BRS Meat Haulage.

Pickfords Heavy Haulage dealt with abnormal loads. This 1945 Scammell 'CD' 45 ton tractor had just delivered a 75 ton hydraulic press, assisted by a World War 2 Diamond T. (Photo: Vauxhall Motors Ltd)

mainly Leyland Beavers and trailers while its local dock to market outfits consisted of Bedford 'S' type and Austin Series 3 ballasted tugs with Dyson trailers. Other makes on journey work included Maudslay and AEC.

In the immediate post war period, the British commercial vehicle industry began to re-establish itself after five years of concerted military vehicle and armament production. Most of its capacity had been switched to designing and building armoured vehicles, tanks and essential equipment to aid the war effort. Certain manufacturers had been permitted to produce civilian vehicles which were much needed along with those for the Forces. Civilian heavies came from Atkinson, Foden, ERF and Maudslay during the war, mostly in austere war-time guise without their normal polished radiators and chromed headlamps, windscreen surrounds and wheel trims.

With the return of peace new model ranges were planned while pre-war models were temporarily retained in production. The first post-war Commercial Motor Show at Earls Court in 1948 saw the introduction of many new models. Notable types were ERF's 'Streamline' range and Foden's 'S18' cabbed models, both of which had shaken off the war-time drabness. Leyland were well ahead with their new post-war 'O.600' engined range as early as 1946. A much modernised flush- fronted cab graced the Beaver, Steer, Hippo and Octopus covering gross weights of 12, 15, 19 and 22 tons, each being designed for trailer work.

AEC, Albion, Atkinson, Scammell and Thornycroft were more conservative in appearance, so too were some of the lighter trucks from Austin, Bedford, Ford, Morris Commercial, Seddon and Vulcan, which differed only slightly from their pre-war counterparts. Newcomers to the diesel scene were Sentinel's tastefully styled 'DV' models, initially in the form of the 7/8 ton payload 4/4DV. The handsome lines of Sentinel's cab embodied the spirit of the period.

Under Government restrictions, aimed to boost export performance, manufacturers were only allowed

Tasteful styling which embodied the spirit of post-war vehicle design. The Sentinel underfloor-engined range brought new elegance into cab styling. (Photo: R. Woodvine collection)

to sell so many vehicles on the home market. 60% of production had to be sold for export. Whilst this target was soon reached the policy imposed difficulties on transport firms who wanted to improve their fleets and invest in new rolling stock.

At least the export drive succeeded in putting British lorries on the world map. With its accessible market in the Commonwealth combined with a concerted drive in Europe, whose own industries were of course also suffering from the aftermath of war, Britain soon reached record export levels.

In 1948 exports were five times those of 1938 and by 1952 this figure had doubled to ten times the pre-war figure. The tough conditions encountered in some developing countries demanded new levels of engineering – more powerful engines able to withstand extremes of climate; longer service life; higher reliability – all of which had spin off for the home buyer. Britain became the world's leading truck producer and remained so throughout the fifties.

In spite of the massive export achievement that had taken place by 1950 the budget in April of that year came as a blow to the industry with purchase tax up to 33$\frac{1}{3}$% on new vehicles together with a massive increase in fuel tax. The chief aim of this was to curb home demand further so that an even bigger proportion of production went to export. Purchase tax was not removed from new commercial vehicles until 1959.

Because of new vehicle shortages British hauliers, even the giant BRS itself, were forced to keep elderly machines in operation on a 'make do and mend' basis as they had done during the war. But, eventually, home supplies began to improve in the early fifties. In 1951 Leyland Motors took large orders for the top of the range Octopus eight wheeler from BRS, up to 300 vehicles at a time. BRS also placed large orders for the AEC Mammoth Major Mk III, ERF 6.8, Albion HD57, Maudslay Meritor and Foden FG6/15 of the same period. The AECs had a mixture of cabs, while the Meritors mainly had cabs built by Oswald Tillotson of Burnley. The majority of the ERFs featured pressed steel 'Willenhall' cabs.

Until the advent of articulation in the late fifties rigid eight wheelers were the mainstay of the long distance trunk operation. The more powerful makes, especially the Leyland Octopus and AEC Mammoth Major models frequently drew eight ton four wheel drawbar trailers, largely of Dyson origin.

Such was the importance of the eight wheeler to the BRS operations that this type was chosen as the 'standard' maximum capacity vehicle which was put into production by the Bristol Tramways & Carriage Company in 1952. Production of the 'HG6L' model as it was known continued until 1957 during which time 517 were built solely to the order of British Road Services. All had Leyland 'O.600' diesel engines developing 125 brake horse power.

One clear effect of Labour's nationalisation was the

disappearance of hundreds of celebrated transport fleets with their individually liveried lorries. For a while one could see familiar lorries from well known fleets like W. H. Bowker still carrying their old colours, but with 'Penelope' the lion superimposed on their cab doors. BRS inherited a wide variety of ageing trucks, many of them pre-war and nearing the end of their useful lives. They ranged from Armstrong Saurers and early thirties petrol-engined AECs to vintage bonneted Scammell articulated eight wheelers and Yorkshire 'WK6' diesels. It was only when the industry picked up and new machines became available that BRS could place their orders for new rigid eights to put on trunk operations where reliability was so important.

The stamp of state control. This Atkinson of W H Bowker has received its BRS roundels but still wears its pre-nationalisation livery. (Photo: A J Ingram)

Alongside those who avidly followed developments in the world of state ownership were those who looked on the vanishing individuality of the forties with leaden heart. While some of the pre-nationalisation names were re-born in 1953 and 1954 after the Road Haulage Disposal Board broke up BRS, gone forever were those magnificent Scammell 'Showboats' belonging to Fisher Renwick of Manchester and London, and those of Young's Express Deliveries of Paisley. Britain's trunk roads had also seen the last of such illustrious names as Bouts Tillotson Transport, Northumbrian Transport Services Ltd, Teeside Motor Transfer of Middlesbrough, General Roadways of London, H. & G. Dutfield Ltd, J. Baxter Transport of Newcastle on Tyne, Northern Despatch Motor Company, Currie & Company, Edward Box, Southern Roadways and many more.

If one fleet truly symbolised the late forties it was that of Fisher Renwick who ran the great Scammell eight wheeler 'Showboats' on regular trunk services between Manchester and London and between

Few lorries have ever rivalled the charismatic Fisher Renwick 'show-boats' – they have a special place in British transport history. (Photo: Ted Oates collection)

Manchester and Glasgow. Manchester-born Ted Oates who has spent his life in road haulage, first as driver and later as Transport Manager of an own-account fleet, remembers riding on the Fisher Renwick Scammells as a boy. His father, Jimmy, was one of the regular night men who drove on the Manchester to London run.

As Ted recalls, up to a dozen lorries loaded during the day at the White City depot, would set out from Manchester at around seven in the evening. They would head out along the A56 Chester road bound for Stonebridge in Staffordshire, via Altrincham and Knutsford. At Stonebridge they would meet to exchange lorries with the night men who had come up from London. The 'change-over' system enabled the drivers to return home by the end of their driving hours.

The scene at 'Ma's', the regular change-over point at Bacon End on the A452 near Stonebridge, must have exceeded the wildest dreams of any lorry enthusiast. While the drivers supped welcome cups of tea, up to 20 or 30 wagons could be lined up on the roadside.

Dimly lit by their cab lights and side lamps they presented a wonderful spectacle against the blackness of the night. There were Scammells, ERFs and Maudslays, some with van bodies and others with sheeted loads. After exchanging paperwork the drivers took over their opposite number's lorry. Then the stillness of the night would erupt with the thunder of Gardners drowning the parting comments as the drivers set off on their homeward journeys.

Every so often drivers were required to take their loads straight through to London, which meant a night out. Ted recalls one of the better class of 'digs' at the London end was the San Marina, at Bignell's corner on the A6/A1 junction near South Mimms. Once a hotel, it still boasted its own swimming pool. The lorry park, which was usually packed at night, had the benefit of a

pronounced slope which enabled those with starter problems, and the few who did not even have the luxury of a self starter, to roll start their wagons in the morning. Typical of these, as Ted recalls, were Manchester based Radcliffe & Sackville's old DG Foden four wheeler and trailer outfits. Thoughtful 'regulars' would leave them room to drive round and stop at the top of the slope for the morning start-up routine. Swinging a heavy oil engine was no fun and it usually took a rope and one or two muscular helpers to coax it into life.

A similar service to that of Fisher Renwick's was operated by Young's Express Deliveries of Paisley, Glasgow. Their fleet, also predominantly Scammell but featuring a number of Fodens and Albions, also ran nightly trunk services. Resplendent in dark green and red the Young's vehicles would be seen every night along with those of Fisher Renwick's grinding slowly over Shap Fell between Kendal and Penrith on the A6.

An old hand about to demonstrate the technique of swinging an oiler with the aid of a rope.

Shap, in the days when the A6 was just a lonely ribbon of twisting single carriageway, claimed many unfortunate victims in accidents. Steep winding hills called for great care especially with the under-powered and under-braked lorries of the forties. Those who

A T561 Albion 8-wheeled flat of Young's Express Deliveries, Paisley, being loaded in readiness for the night trunk.

chose to coast on downhill stretches sometimes paid dearly for it. The temptation to knock the gear stick into neutral (popularly called 'Aberdeen overdrive' or 'Scotchman's fifth' by some drivers of the period) to gain more speed was always present. On a steady descent a slow-revving diesel would soon be on over-run, holding you back while the footbrake and hand or 'side' brake would have to be used frequently to prevent engine overspeed.

Short spells of coasting in neutral gave welcome relief from the deafening noise as you sailed along in eerie silence. But woe to the driver who had to slow down unexpectedly for there was little chance of that with fifteen to twenty tons of load pushing you along at forty five to fifty miles an hour.

Braking was a weak point on many lorries of the forties and fifties. Whilst some manufacturers like AEC and Thornycroft favoured air pressure braking which was more reliable and easier to maintain, many makes relied on hydraulically actuated brakes. ERF CI6.8 and Atkinson L1586 models had vacuum servo assisted cam brakes with external wheel cylinders. While Atkinson stuck to that type, ERF changed to wedge expanders when they launched the 6.8 'Streamline', in line with the practise of Leyland and Maudslay. Leyland featured vacuum servo assistance whilst ERF and Maudslay

opted for a system which sounded good in theory but proved less than successful in practice. Both had a 'continuous-flow' pressure system which relied on a gearbox driven pump. It provided adequate servo assistance whilst travelling at normal road speeds but performance fell off badly at low speeds as the pump slowed down in accordance with the prop shaft. Needless to say when manoeuvring a heavily laden vehicle about on sloping ground only the strongest legged of drivers could hope to pull up.

Driver's eye view of the A6 through Cumbria in the pre motorway days.

Maudslay, according to ex-Service Manager Harry Pick, were forced by the number of operator complaints to modify many of their Meritor eight wheelers by the fitment of 'air-bag' accumulators and subsequently some were completely re-equipped with full vacuum servo systems. Those that had air-bag accumulators fitted proved to be troublesome from the servicing viewpoint.

The air-bag accumulator worked on the principle that the bag, housed inside a cylinder, became compressed by the hydraulic fluid under pressure and as the pump slowed down the airbag took over providing temporary assistance while the pump pressure was inadequate. Once the speed increased the pump would take over again and the air-bag would become compressed ready for the next time that it was needed.

Every month the air-bag was supposed to be re-inflated as it tended to lose pressure with time. If it was not re-inflated the fluid level in the reserve tank appeared to drop and quite naturally this would be topped up. This resulted in an excess build-up of fluid in the system eventually causing a solid lock-up. The worst was yet to come, when the enormous pressure build-up would cause sudden blow-back through the reserve tank showering the inside of the cab and the unfortunate driver in brake fluid.

From 1952 ERF also fitted an accumulator to get better low speed performance but they used a spring type which was more reliable and needed less attention. Small wonder that by the late fifties heavy vehicle manufacturers were moving over to air-operated 'S-cam' brakes.

Ever conscious of impending disaster the hapless lorry driver of the forties and fifties got used to taking extreme care on downhill stretches. It was customary to slow the lorry to walking pace at the top of a steep hill, drop it down into a lower gear and creep down as gently as possible. If you were pulling a trailer it was even more important to take it easy although the second man with the trailer brake lever on the other side of the cab provided some additional retardation.

If going down hill had its anxious moments then the same could be said for going up. By modern standards the old trucks were seriously under-powered. Even the heaviest of models could only boast around a 120 bhp and with that you could be asked to move 32 tons. AECs and Leylands were among the more powerful vehicles of the period so they were more popular on trailer work than their Foden, ERF and Atkinson counterparts all of which had the 112 bhp Gardner 6LW.

When you did encounter a steep bank nifty down-changes were a must if you were not to grind to an unseemly halt. To get most lorries into 'crawler' you had to lift the stick as you pushed it across the gate and hope that you could engage gear and re-engage the clutch before you lost all momentum.

Even the lighter trucks that were around in the forties were a handful on hills. On top of having inadequate power it was customary to double and sometimes treble the load and get to your destination on a prayer and a song.

Derek 'Bonny' Bonfield from Eaton Bray near Dunstable recalled one occasion immediately after the war when he had a 1938 Bedford WT type 3-tonner on bricks from the Marston Valley Brick Company. Wartime stockpiles of bricks were being used up and it was usual, so 'Bonny' recalls, to load three and a half thousand bricks on the Bedford (a mere 8 tons) which the old faithful WT coped with admirably. With old bricks, prone to be heavier through being damp, he cautiously told the loaders to leave it at three thousand, to avoid too big a load. He was mildly surprised when the loaded WT topped the scales at 12½ tons.

The Bedford WT would rise to almost any challenge. Each of these Aberdeen based vehicles is carrying an 8 ton block of granite. (Photo: Vauxhall Motors Ltd).

At a guess this WT trailer outfit must be grossing about 12 tons. It made daily trips over the Pennines from Manchester to South Yorkshire. (Photo: Vauxhall Motors Limited).

Undaunted, 'Bonny' set out for his destination of Haslemere near High Wycombe. Turning left out of the brickworks he began the gradual climb towards Woburn. A mile or so further on at Husborne Crawley he was still in second gear. In his mind he was planning the best route to avoid any steep hills. He paused just outside High Wycombe at the top of a long descent which bottomed out and began a steep climb up the opposite side of the valley.

Having established from a passer-by that the site was up the hill on the opposite side, he set off in fine style down the hill and as soon as he hit the uphill section went third! – second! – bottom! in as many seconds but the old WT couldn't take it and ground to a halt.

Two drivers discuss the merits of a brand new 1957 Commer TS3 whilst waiting to load up at the CWS African Oil Mills in Liverpool Docks. In the background stands the Liverpool Overhead Railway structure which was demolished in the late fifties.

Heaving frantically at his handbrake 'Bonny' was unable to stop the loaded Bedford creeping back against both the brakes and the engine compression. Spotting a couple of roadside trees through his back window he reversed into them and the lorry rested there precariously whilst he piled a few bricks under the back wheels. He went on foot up to the site, where he slipped a ten shilling note to the driver of a new Bedford O-type who came down to his rescue and double-headed him up the hill!

Until April 1955 the legal gross weight on a four-wheeler was 12 tons. Most 12 ton GVW heavies 'tared' at 4 tons leaving about 8 tons recommended payload. In 1955 the legal GVW was raised to 14 tons and again to 16 tons in 1964.

Individual manufacturers designed their trucks for specific gross weights. For instance, a Seddon Mk 5L had a GVW of 10 tons, a Morris Commercial 'FV' or a Bedford 'O' type 8 tons, and so forth. Only the real 'heavies' like Leyland Beavers, AEC Mandators and the like were meant for the full 12 tons. Few small operators of the time really paid any heed to this and indeed most manufacturers designed with the knowledge that overloading was likely.

Regardless of make or type it was pretty normal, and incidentally quite legal, to top the 12 to 14 ton mark gross on the weighbridge otherwise the payload did not pay so well. Skilful driving usually avoided mishaps caused through overloading, although there were times when brakes, tyres, and half-shafts could not cope.

Until the advent of annual MoT testing, maintenance often left much to be desired. According to Bob Rust, a professional lorry driver for 35 years, there was one famous London based firm who, when visited by a the local vehicle examiner, were asked to show him their maintenance facilities. He was directed to a cobbled side street in dockland where various ageing eight wheelers stood partly dismantled. Asked if this was where they did their maintenance he was told "we only mend them when they goes wrong and then we don't mend them much".

One of that very firm's Leyland eight wheelers was up on a jack on the side of the A6 at Bletsoe, north of Bedford, one afternoon when local lad Pete Smith, now an owner-driver, strolled down from his house nearby to take a closer look. The lorry had suffered a front wheel blow-out on the S-bend by the Falcon Inn and the company breakdown truck had come out with assistance.

Leaning against the lorry was a ten stud 40x8 wheel and tyre with patches of canvas where the tread should be. "No wonder it went" observed Pete. The driver shook his head "No son, that's the new one they have just brought out to me".

The desperate measures resorted to in war when tyres were virtually unobtainable, seemed acceptable in the circumstances, and it took a while for the peace-time standards of safety to become re-established.

New vehicle shortages led many hauliers to purchase re-worked ex-army trucks. It was reckoned that an army truck rated at 3 tons was good for 7 or more in civvy street. Some intriguing conversions were put to work in the forties and fifties.

Toddington, near Dunstable, was the base for Candelent's fleet of ex-Army Bedfords. One-time Candelent driver Derek Itsinger recalls that the twenty-strong fleet included eight artics which were remarkable in that they were made from QL 4x4s converted to 4x2s and hitched to fifth wheel semi trailers. They were shortened, their 28hp petrol engines replaced by Perkins P6 diesels and their front axles replaced by Thornycroft units from the military 3-ton 'Sturdy'. They worked out of the local brickworks at Stewartby on long distance, returning with various goods including foodstuffs and animal feed from the docks. Ex US Army 25ft semi trailers were used, having Westinghouse air brakes and Trilex pattern wheels. Candelent's artics were an impressive sight in their green and silver livery. It was standard procedure for every vehicle to carry a tow pole and a spare halfshaft as a routine precaution!

Another extraordinary creation which was based for some years at Leighton Buzzard, was a hybrid Albion rigid 8 wheeler. H. G. Pentus-Brown, a leading haulier in the region, remembers how his fitters converted a

World War 2 bonneted Albion CX22 heavy artillery tractor into a long wheelbase rigid 8. The 8ft 9in wide tractors rarely got used except as recovery vehicles since they were over the legal width of 7ft 6in. Pentus-Brown's 'CX' was bought from Elstow in 1946 with only 3000 miles on the clock. It was too good not to use, so 'Pentus' and his workshop boffins decided to carry out a major conversion.

The tractor was lengthened to take a 24ft body, the front axle was 'cut and shut' to bring it down to legal width, 36x8 wheels and tyres were fitted, a second steering axle was added and the driving position was changed to forward control, using a cab from an ex-London Transport AEC tower wagon. Low gearing made the vehicle too slow so 'Pentus' decided to turn the 2-speed auxiliary gearbox round, so that it provided an overdrive and thus the 'Bitza' Albion went to work. In its 'Fletton Bricks' livery of dark blue it worked out of Water Eaton near Bletchley for many years clocking over 200,000 miles. The ultimate fate of this machine is uncertain but Bletchley haulier Bert Winkfield distinctly remembers it still at work in 1958.

Of all the varied kinds of transport operation, none have quite the mystique and lore of the long distance trunk service. In essence the 'trunk' is a regular inter-city service where the vehicles are loaded by day and the loaded vehicle travels by night to its destination, returning the following night having been unloaded and reloaded by the day man or shunt driver.

Noteworthy trunk operators of the fifties were Sutton and Son Ltd of St. Helens, W. H. Bowker Ltd of Blackburn, Richardson's (Hull) Transport, Harrison's of Dewsbury, Hanson's of Huddersfield, Buckley's of Warrington, J & A Smith of Maddiston, Hill's of Cardiff, Ross Garages and numerous others in the 'big league'.

Perhaps the biggest difference between operations in the fifties and those of today is the much greater distance now possible in one shift.

Before motorways came into being the routes took in many large towns and villages and main roads were largely single-carriageway with steep hills, narrow bridges, tight bends and road junctions. Coupled with this the legal speed limit was 20 mph on heavy lorries until 1957.

Nowadays a northbound trunk, leaving London via the M1 and M6 would be very nearly in Birmingham in the time it took the lumbering trunkers of the fifties to reach Dunstable on the old A5. Consequently the drivers could be 'out of hours' after only 250 miles or so. In fact London to Liverpool was a typical night's work for a trunker in the fifties. Today this distance can easily be accomplished, plus the return journey to London, without exceeding the driver's hours.

Chris Gardner, who is currently Depot Manager at W.H.Bowker of Blackburn, described the trunk operations in the days of Leyland Octopus and Guy eight wheelers, when Bowker's were one of the leading fruit hauliers. Fully laden lorries would be awaiting the

night men at Blackburn and Liverpool depots when they booked on in the early evening. The lorries would be loaded with a mixture of goods, possibly paper or foodstuffs. They would have been neatly sheeted and roped by day men, 'juiced up' with DERV, and generally checked over. By 7 o'clock the trunk drivers (who probably had the easier of the two jobs) were making a final check around their tyres, lights and loads, before setting out for London.

There were no motorways, so the route from Blackburn went through Bolton and Manchester before joining the A556 to Knutsford via Altrincham. Meanwhile the Liverpool vehicles headed for Knutsford on the A50 through Warrington. From Knutsford the A50 took them on to Holmes Chapel to join the A34 via Talke Bank and Stoke on Trent. The A34 took them down to Two Gates on the A5 through Stone, Rugeley and Litchfield.

Once on the A5 they pressed on towards Hinckley and Crick, stopping for a break at a roadside cafe. The A5 continued towards Dunstable and St. Albans where the A6 and A1 took them into London by about 6 o'clock in the morning.

Having been loaded by the day shunters, two of Bowker's long-distance 'trunkers' await the nightmen at the London depot. (Photo: A. J. Ingram).

Conditions varied considerably of course at different times of the year, but the service had to go on regardless of weather. On a summer's evening there would be two hours or more of daylight left and only six hours or so of darkness before you were enjoying the splendour of the dawn sky along relatively deserted roads. Winter meant 11 hours of darkness made worse by cold cabs and treacherous weather conditions.

The first break for the drivers, around midnight, would probably see them at the 'Rendezvous' cafe – time for a hot cup of tea and a chat with the other drivers and, perhaps, to get their heads down for a few minutes nap. Then it was time to press on through the night, meeting a few familiar lorries on their northbound journey.

After eleven hours at the wheel, our drivers would have completed their early morning stint through

North London, mingling with other night trunkers and milk floats on their rounds. The Metropolis would be just coming to life when the lorries pulled into the North London depot for the day shunters to take over.

It was the job of the shunt drivers to take the lorries on to their final destinations and unload them. Next stage was to make for Covent Garden where the fruit orders would be wheeled out and loaded. Shunters had the hard work of loading and sheeting, which was usually completed by late afternoon so that the lorries were back at the depot ready for the night men to take over once again.

They would usually set out around 7 pm. on their return journey to Liverpool, Blackburn, Manchester or Preston, to complete the cycle.

Articulation was beginning to gain popularity by the late fifties. One advantage of this was that the night trunk could be run on a 'change-over' system in which trailers would be swapped at a convenient half way stage, usually a cafe lorry park, enabling the night men to return home in their own tractor units. This saved staying away in digs. Trailers could also be dropped at customers' loading bays while the units were utilised elsewhere.

At first Artics had no payload advantage over rigid eights, the average semi-trailer was only about 24 feet long and the legal gross weight was only 24 tons.

The windscreen of Harrison's of Dewsbury's AEC trailer outfit has an all important clean-up prior to leaving London on its night trunk to South Yorkshire.

The half-hitch or 'dolly' is the lorry driver's special knot for tensioning ropes. Roping is fast becoming a rarity in many branches of transport as curtain-siders gain popularity.

'Benders' as they were christened, presented the 'rigid' drivers with quite a challenge when it came to reversing. Even experienced men had to re-learn their trade if they came off rigids on to artics. With little, short wheelbase tractors they were also prone to jack-knifing on slippery surfaces. The only widely seen artics in the forties and fifties were the famous Scammell 'Eight Wheelers', forerunners of the 'Highwayman'.

Whatever the type of lorry – four, six or eight wheeler, rigid or artic, life in the cab was much the same – hot in summer, cold in winter, noisy all year round.

Cabs were primitive by modern standards – shaky constructions from wood and aluminium, with hard non-adjustable seats and enormous four spoke steering wheels. Strong arm muscles were a must and a strong left leg too to work the clutch. Instruments and switchgear consisted of the bare minimum.

Headlights were used only in pitch darkness. It was customary to see lorries running on side and tail lights well into the gathering dusk and in the half light of dawn. Sometimes on moonlit nights headlights were not used at all except as signals to other drivers.

A well practised code of headlamp flashes served as a rudimentary communication system before Citizen's Band came into being. You could signal 'hello', 'thanks', 'you are clear to pass', 'after you', 'watch it, the law's down the road', or 'careful, accident ahead' and make yourself understood.

For instance if you were gaining on a slower lorry in front, at night, you'd give a single off-on with the headlights. If it was clear, the lorry in front would give you a couple of dips on the headlights and on you went, watching in your mirror for a single long off-on with the headlights to show you it was clear to pull in. Then you replied with a short and a long on-off with your rear lamps to say thanks. Repeated on-off switching of your side and tail meant you were about to turn off the main road. Several flashes on the headlights to an on-coming lorry meant 'warning, danger ahead'.

The switchgear on many heavies was well positioned down to the right of the driver's seat where the large toggle switches were easy to feel. The Simms 'DQ' control box on the Octopus and some AECs was especially convenient. Many AECs had the big CAV boxes with top-mounted switches which were heavier in action.

There was something to be said for cab designs of the fifties. In a peculiar way they offered a better environment than some modern cabs. They were somehow friendlier than the high-tech creations of the eighties. Driving positions, especially on the AECs were very commanding even though tall drivers complained of the lowness of the roof line which called for a hunched driving posture. But on hot days you could open the windscreen for some fresh air. If you had cramp in your left leg (from working that heavy clutch) you could stretch it out over the engine cover. With only a speedo', an oil and an air gauge to worry about the instrumentation was easily checked and the stately pace enabled you to enjoy the scenery or to count the 'cats eyes'.

AEC cab interior from the fifties. Such spartan conditions would not bear comparison with today's luxurious cabs. Main fuel filter (not visible here) was bolted to front panel opposite the mate's seat, so cabs usually smelt of fuel oil. Thirties AECs had an Autovac in this position.

If anything, noise was the greatest drawback. Engine covers rarely sealed off properly, and even generous layers of coats, sacks and carpet off-cuts did little to dull the penetrating roar of the oil engine hammering away hour after hour. If some may have delighted to the sound of a diesel doing ten to the bar, most heaved a sigh of relief when they operated the stop control.

Throughout the thirty odd years since the end of the 1950s there has been sweeping progress in almost every aspect of road transport. Much of the hard graft of manual loading and sheeting has given way to pre-loaded containers and mechanical handling; those noisy cramped cabs have been developed into spacious 'flight decks' with luxury car comfort; strict annual testing of trucks has more or less stamped out bad maintenance and motorways with modern truckstops have replaced the treacherous old routes with their 'greasy spoon' style cafes.

The forties and fifties are now just memories, but oddly enough there are many who cannot look back on those years without some feeling of nostalgia. ■

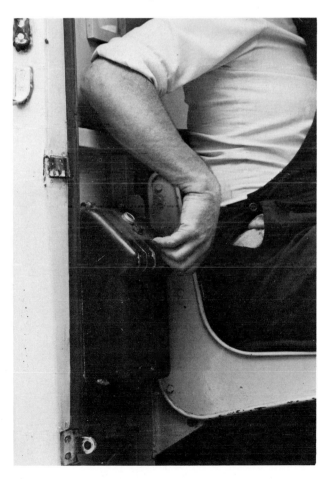

Convenient – the positive and well placed toggle switches of the Simms 'DQ' control box, as fitted to Leyland '600' series. Household type fuses could be easily reached and repaired in seconds using standard fuse wire.

FOUR WHEELERS

Unlike 6 or 8-wheeled rigids, four-wheelers span a wide range of sizes, weights and types. For the purpose of this book, a 4-wheeled lorry is any 2 axled load carrier for a payload of 2 tons and over, although the main emphasis is on heavier vehicles of 5 to 8 tons payload.

During the forties and early fifties the gross weight limit for four-wheelers was 12 tons. From April 1955 a four-wheeler could gross at 14 tons and the width and length limits of 7ft 6in by 27ft 6in became 8ft by 30ft.

Four-wheelers have always had an important role to play and they form the major part of our lorry population. Most goods are moved in relatively small consignments over short distances. For such work large multi-wheelers would have no benefit.

Nowadays most four-wheelers are of the forward control layout, but in the forties and fifties bonneted vehicles were still favoured for multi-drop distribution work. Modern day easy-access forward control cabs make the driver's job easier and allow more body length. Before manufacturers like Bedford, Ford and Austin offered forward control models some operators had bonneted models converted. Leading specialists in this field were G. R. Neville of Mansfield who overcame resulting engine access problems by fitting tilt cabs.

In the forties and fifties there were two distinct classes of truck, identifiable by their pricing. There were the mass-produced low-cost products and the premium quality heavily-engineered machines. While Austin, Bedford and Ford offered 7-tonners for around the £1,000 mark, the Leyland, ERF, Foden and Atkinson equivalents would cost over twice that. This 'quality gap' has diminished over the years.

In theory the cheaper products were built for a shorter life, for a proportionately lower outlay, but low priced parts and maintenance sometimes made them a more profitable proposition than their quality built rivals.

British lorry of the forties and fifties – the Sentinel 4/4DV. Built at Shrewsbury in the heart of Britain between 1946 & 1956, they were powered by a well engineered 6.08 litre, horizontal 4-cylinder diesel engine. The first ones had the 4SRH2 Ricardo indirect injection engines giving 90bhp at 2000 rpm. From 1952 onwards the 4SDH direct injection engine was fitted, which was slower revving and gave 80bhp at 1800 rpm. These solidly built 7/8-tonners featured Kirkstall axles, David Brown gearboxes and Lockheed 'continuous flow' hydraulic braking. 'OFM 50' dates from 1951.

AEC Monarch Mk IIIs had the 7.7 litre diesel with its chain-driven timing. They were built from 1945 to 1956 and were a low weight 8-tonner. The very first new AEC to be delivered after the war was a Monarch Mk III which went to Aberford Motor Company.

Similar in appearance to the Monarch Mk III, the Mandator Mk III was powered by the bigger 9.6 litre diesel making it suitable for trailer work. The earlier equivalent was called the Matador but during the war this title was bestowed on the 4-wheel-drive military MAT (medium artillery tractor). This Mandator served in the fleet of Henry Long Transport of Bradford on wool traffic, hence the rack extension over the cab.

Introduced in late 1953, the low-weight AEC Mercury, produced at the Maudslay plant in Great Alne, near Alcester, brought a new look to AECs with its flush mounted head-lamps and wide dummy radiator grille. Park Royal Vehicles supplied most of the cabs but there were numerous other bodybuilders such as Duramin, Holmes and Bowyer Bros. At 12 tons gvw the Mercury was a full 8-tonner powered by the new AV410 diesel of 98bhp. A larger engine, the 125bhp AV470, was also available.

Albions retained their vintage appearance in the early post-war years. This FT3AL model dates from 1949. They had a 4.25 litre, 6-cylinder petrol engine developing 80bhp.

Advertised as 'Knights of the Road', Atkinson lorries, from their factory at Winery Lane Preston, had an excellent reputation for solid British engineering. Almost invariably powered by Gardner they featured proprietary mechanical units from Kirkstall and David Brown in much the same tradition as ERF and Maudslay. This L745 dates from 1951.

Right: The classic 'Atki' 4-wheeler of the period could be ordered from a choice of 4, 5 or 6 cylinder models – all Gardner powered. They were slow but reliable and characterised the solid British workmanship of the fifties. British Leather of Birkenhead operated this 1951 example.

Below, Left to right:
Underfloor engines were being considered by several manufacturers in the fifties. Sentinel were the leading exponents. Albion, Commer, Atkinson and Rowe-Hillmaster also featured them. Among the best remembered 'underfloor' lorries were the 'Claymores' from Albion. A horizontal 4.1 litre 4-cylinder diesel powered the later 4/5-tonners which were popular in distribution fleets. This one only just qualifies for inclusion in this book as it was built in late '59.

Indestructible. When it comes to solid, high quality engineering, Foden's famous 'DG' range took some beating. By the time they were replaced in the late forties by the FG and FE range they were looking extremely dated, the basic design having been launched in the mid thirties. Gardner oil engines powered all DG models (the G standing for 'Gardner') but other components were of Foden's design and manufacture.

Known as the 'Interim' Beaver and designated 12.IB., this 8.6 litre diesel-powered 7-tonner bore some resemblance to the pre-war range. The cab was similar to that of the wartime military Hippo. The engine was basically as that of the Matilda tank. 12.IBs were built in 1946 prior to the launch of the new '600' range.

Dating from 1950 this Austin 'K2' 2-tonner, seen here in horsebox form, had a 4 litre 6-cylinder petrol engine and, along with the Bedford M-type, was a popular light truck in the forties and fifties.

Austin moved into forward control in 1955 to meet the growing demand for longer bodywork. Normal control trucks, which were popular in distribution fleets, usually had bodies around 14 feet long. Some were converted to forward control to gain an extra two feet or so of body space. The cab for the Austin 'Series 3' 5-tonner was bought in from the Willenhall Motor Radiator Company. Originally introduced in 1954, it was fitted to the first FVS Morris Commercials and to ERFs. It also went on Guy and Dennis lorries of the fifties. On the right is another 'Series 3' photographed in 1955, just three years after Austin and Morris joined up to form the British Motor Corporation.

26

Bedford's first civilian forward control truck was the 7-ton 'S' type or 'Big Bedford' as it was dubbed by the marketing men. A completely new design concept for Vauxhall Motors, it appeared to borrow something of the trans-Atlantic styling from its parent company's GMC trucks of the period. Originally it had a 110bhp 6-cylinder petrol engine. Growing demand for diesel power saw the option of a Perkins R6 in 1953 and, in 1958, Bedford's own '300' diesel. In petrol form the 'S' type could be bodied under 3 tons unladen weight and could legally operate at 30mph instead of 20. The 20 limit was lifted in 1955. The 'S' type range was discontinued in late 1959.

Also reminiscent of American design was the Bedford 'D' type of 1957. It was a short-lived development of the 'A' type and was built for only one year prior to the introduction of the TJ range. Payload ratings ranged from 1½-tons up to 6-tons and petrol or diesel power was offered, the diesel still being regarded as optional equipment.

'Big Sister' to the 'Series 3' opposite was BMC's '701' 7-tonner which appeared in 1957. It was powered by the 5.1 litre diesel engine and was a rival to the Bedford 'S' type in the low cost, mass-produced world of trucks. Although they did much the same job as Fodens, ERFs and Leylands there was thought to be a quality gap in the British truck market – something which has now disappeared.

Exceptionally modern in looks and general design when it was launched in 1948, the Commer 'QX' was a mass-produced 5/7-tonner, later to face competition from Ford, Bedford and BMC. Initially it was powered by the 4.75 litre underfloor 6-cylinder petrol engine. In 1954 it was given the highly unconventional Rootes 3-cylinder, opposed-piston, horizontal 2-stroke diesel, which will always be remembered for its unmistakable sound. This 1956 TS3 diesel operated in the large fleet of London based grocery and provision merchants, Kearley and Tongue Ltd.

Above: ERF were soon to launch their new 'Streamline' series when this 1945 4-wheeler was built. The prefix 'CI' meaning 'compression ignition', another term for diesel, was still in use. 4-wheelers were CI4.4, CI5.4, or CI6.4 depending on whether they had a 4, 5 or 6-cylinder engine.

Left: When BRS ordered new ERFs they specified the Willenhall steel cab in preference to the Jennings coach built version. This South Leeds group vehicle is so equipped. The Jennings cabs lasted longer as they were less susceptible to corrosion.

Opposite:

Top: This 1946 Dennis Pax has no pretensions about following the new styling trends of the post war years. The Guildford-built 5/6-tonner was typical of the rather staid designs of the thirties and forties but, old fashioned or not, it was a well thought out design, featuring an easy-to-enter cab.

Lower left: Standard power unit for the Dennis Max 8-tonner was their own 4-cylinder 6.5 litre 80bhp diesel. A 7.6 litre 6-cylinder version was also available giving 100bhp. The Max had its origins in the thirties and was decidedly dated when it was replaced by the more modern Condor model in 1957.

Lower right: Dubbed the 'Parrot Nose' this 1954 Dodge 'Kew' 7-tonner shared the same basic Briggs Motor Bodies cab as the Ford Thames ET6 and the Leyland Comet. Under the bonnet was a Perkins R6 diesel.

Foden's S18 'Saloon' cab was yet another product of the peacetime revival of innovative design. Like ERFs, Foden's FG models might have 4, 5, or 6-cylinder Gardners under their bonnets and from the outside it was difficult to tell which. There was no doubt if the Foden was an 'FE' with their own 2-stroke engine since it heralded its approach with an incomparable howling sound.

Britain's thrust into the world markets after the war encouraged more adventurous cab styling. The normal control Comet from Leyland is an example. Originally launched in 1948 as the Comet '75' with the 305 cu.in. (5 litre) diesel it became the Comet '90' in 1952, when the O.351 diesel became standard. When first launched, there was also a petrol engined version. This photograph shows a 1956 Comet 90, from the Manbre and Garton Fleet.

Leyland's forward control or 'side' type Comet which was launched in 1953, was fitted with a version of the later '600' series steel cab, examples of which appear on pages 45 and 64. There were however, alternative cabs available from proprietary bodybuilders. On the left is a 1955 model with an unusual Holmes light alloy cab. This vehicle was operated by J.D.James from Tregaron in Mid-Wales. Driver Ieuan Evans is taking a break en-route from Liverpool to Tregaron with a load of animal feed.

Another variation on the Comet cab theme – this one is from Bonallack, who set the headlamps closer together than others. This 1955 dropside was used on the transport of steel forgings between Sheffield and Luton. With its Albion 5-speed box and Eaton 2-speed axle, the Comet could comfortably top 60 mph.

On the less-than-glamorous urban delivery work, Morris Commercial 'CV' models were a popular choice along with their Bedford, Thames and Austin counterparts. The 'CV' had a choice of 4 or 6-cylinder petrol engine and differed little from the pre-war model. This 2-tonner with a standard dropside body, dates from 1951.

Top, left to right:
In terms of appearance, Sentinel's 'hinged door' cabs, which were offered as alternatives to the standard versions (see pages 20/21) were a retrograde step. Looks apart, they offered easier access, greater proof against corrosion, easier repair and more room. The standard cab's biggest drawback was its tiny sliding doors which proved awkward, especially for a big built driver.

The Seddon Mk5L was a rugged and willing workhorse pitched between the cheaper mass produced trucks and the expensive premium quality heavies. They were used in large numbers by British Road Services and were powered by the Perkins P6 diesel. This one, belonging to A.P. Salmon, is struggling through the the congested main street of Luton, with a long load of timber for Latham's.

'No frills' sums up the Perkins engined Vulcan 6PF 6-tonner from the late forties. Production of Vulcan lorries ceased in 1952, two years after parent company Tilling Stevens was absorbed into the Rootes Group. They were a typically British creation from the old-established Maidstone based company. This example was captured on film on a wet day along the Liverpool Dock Road.

Right: Thornycroft's 'Nippy Star' and 'Sturdy Star' models were designed for 3/4 ton and 5/6 ton payloads respectively. A choice of 3.8 litre 4 cylinder petrol or 4 litre 6 cylinder diesel was available. This 1950 'Sturdy Star' distributed sterilised milk in the Manchester area.

Every so often a vehicle brings a new image to the truck world. The innovative Foden FE4/8 was one such machine. Powered by the FD4 2.72 litre 2-stroke diesel it marked a departure from Foden's conventional designs, having a 'cab ahead of engine' layout. The ultra-modern walk-through cab by Bowyer seated three in comfort and low steps provided easy access. Surprisingly the cab was not designed to tilt, since the overall layout leant itself to tilting. At 12 tons gvw the FE4/8 could be bodied at just over 3½ tons unladen. It only remained in production for two years.

This Albion FT21 dates from 1947 and was photographed in its home town of Glasgow. Scotland's foremost commercial vehicle manufacturer joined the Leyland Group in 1951. After a proud history the company was slowly wound down and by 1971 the last Albion badged models had been built. Vehicle production ceased altogether in 1980. This picture recalls Albions in their heyday.

Not instantly recognisable as an Austin, this 1955 3-tonner had an unusual bespoke design of cab. It was photographed in the Barnsley area on shop deliveries.

Among the more common delivery vehicles of the fifties, were the Ford Thames 'ET7s'. This was one of a large fleet used to distribute Mothers Pride bread to high street shops throughout the country. They were powered by the 4D 65bhp 3.6 litre 4-cylinder diesel.

Linesmen's vehicles were specialised trucks, purpose-built for GPO telephone maintenance crews. In the pre-Telecom era GPO vehicles were finished in sober dark green and black. This Karrier CK3 dates from 1949 and was powered by an 80bhp 6-cylinder side valve petrol engine.

Right: The dark blue Guy Vixen pantechnicons of Pickfords Removals were a familiar sight in every corner of Britain during the forties and fifties. Pickfords formed part of the BRS Special Traffics Division under nationalisation. Standard power unit for Vixens was a 4-cylinder 3.7 litre petrol developing 58bhp. From 1955 onwards the Perkins P4 was fitted and production ceased in 1964.

Below, left to right:
Integral vans on heavyweight chassis were relatively few but for certain trades they had their advantages. This impressive Leyland Beaver dates from 1957 and was one of a number operated by General Industrial Cleaners from aptly named Borrowash, near Derby. G.I.C. specialised in cleaning industrial workwear.

This 1952 Maudslay Mogul of the Post Office Supplies Department has a slightly unfamiliar appearance resulting from re-positioned headlights. Maudslays were widely used by the GPO in the forties and fifties, the later orders being 'AEC' type with Maudslay badges. Although designated 'Mogul', they were basically the same as the AEC Monarch, with the AEC 7.7 litre diesel. Maudslays also offered a 9.6 engined Mogul similar to the AEC Mandator.

One of Britain's rarer makes was the Rutland, built by Motor Traction of Croydon, between 1952 and 1957. This 1957 Luton van, is probably a '6T714' from the 'Master' range. Rutland offered a wide choice of engines and extensive range of model types throughout their short history.

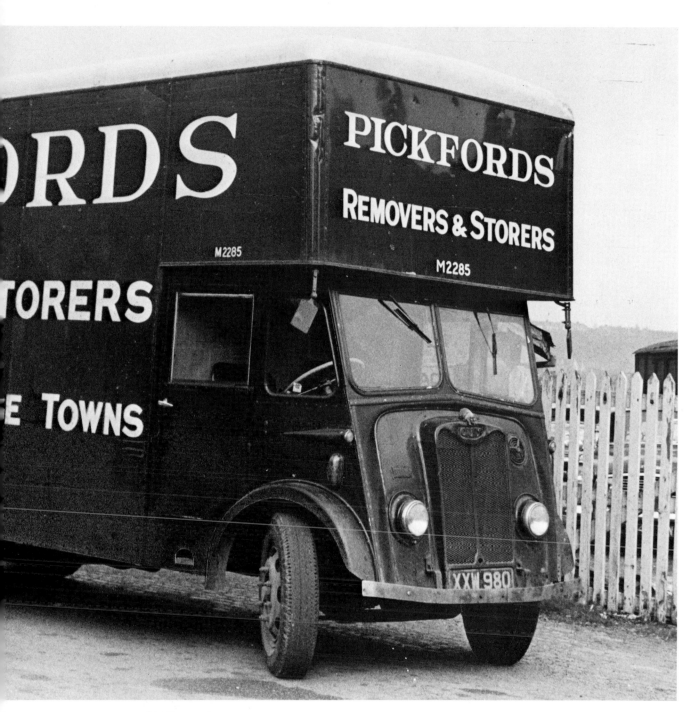

Bedford in wartime 'OW' form with square-nosed bonnet. There were thousands of OWs and their OY military counterparts in use immediately after the war. They were tough workhorses, taking their power from the renowned 28 horsepower 6-cylinder petrol engine.

'Big Bedford' in tanker form. One of a large fleet run by the Esso Petroleum Company. This one was seen parked at their Lampeter depot in Wales. The four-compartment 1500 gallon tank was by Darham Industries.

An early 'flat-front' S18 cab (with the hinged flap for access to the radiator filler) is featured on this 1950 Foden FG5/7½ acid tanker from I.C.I's Mond Division.

A Co-operative Wholesale Society ERF milk tanker unloading at a bottling dairy in Luton. This vehicle has a single compartment 1800 gallon stainless steel tank and a Jennings Streamline cab.

Liquid tar was the load for this 1953 Leyland Comet 90, powered by the 100bhp 5.76 litre O.351 diesel. It was operated by Printar Industries whose headquarters were at Prince Regent's Wharf, Silvertown in East London.

A 1950 Foden FG 5/7½ tanker used to deliver acid to chrome plating works. It was operated by J. B. Ashworth of Horwich near Bolton and was fitted with the early flat-front S18 cab.

Tunnel Refineries of Greenwich operated this 1950 Leyland Beaver 12.B/1, with a smart panelled-in tank body for transporting liquid glucose. It was powered by the 9.8 litre 'O.600' diesel and grossed 12 tons.

Bulk cement deliveries were becoming common-place in the fifties with purpose-built tipping tanks like this one, mounted on a 1958 forward control Leyland Comet. It was based at the Houghton Regis works of Blue Circle Cement.

Two of a large fleet of liquid oxygen tankers run by the British Oxygen Company in the fifties. The 105,000 cu.ft. spherical 'bubble' tanks were built by Blairs of Glasgow. The liquid oxygen was transported at very low temperatures under high pressure. The Sentinel chassis are 4/4DVs with the 90bhp SRH2 horizontal 4-cylinder indirect injection diesel.

Delivering lime to a farm in rural Wales, this Austin normal control '503' 5-ton short wheelbase end tipper was operated by D. J. Herbert of Ammanford in South Wales.

Classic 5-ton tipper of the forties was the Bedford OSBT with factory built body. Using the 28hp petrol engine and four speed crash gearbox they were remarkably rugged, to stand up to tough site work.

Successor to the OSBT was the A5 model, similar in mechanical specification but featuring a synchromesh gearbox and a new cab with a strong American influence in its styling. 'A' Type Bedfords were built from 1953 to 1957.

Top: Largest Bedford tipper in the fifties was the 7-ton SST. This one, registered in 1958, was used by E. Inskip of Bedford and has the standard 6 cu.yd. factory-fitted steel body.

Above left: Morris's rival to the 'S' type tipper was the '7K' 7-tonner with the 5.1 litre 90bhp BMC diesel and featuring a Willenhall cab.

Above: Local Councils liked the 'normal control' style of tipper like this 1949 4-ton Commer Superpoise. It seated the driver and two workmen. It had a 4-litre 6-cylinder petrol.

Left: The Trader 6 cu.yard tipper was popular in its day. With its short 9ft wheelbase and good ground clearance it was well suited to site work. The '6D' 5.4 litre diesel developed 100bhp at 2,500rpm.

With its underfloor 'TS3' power unit, the short wheelbase Commer QX tipper provided a three seater cab. It, too, rivalled the Bedford 'S' type and BMC 7-tonners and offered more power combined with good fuel economy. This example is a 1955 model operated by H. Grace of Bletchley.

When Dodge Brothers entered the forward control class they used the LAD (Leyland-Albion-Dodge) cab, developed by Motor Panels of Coventry. Under the bonnet was a 105bhp Perkins R6. This 1958 7-tonner was operated on the transport of sand and gravel by Conways of Rushden.

Top: Heavily engineered 7/8-ton tippers like this 1946 ERF carried the same payload as mass-produced versions but were generally expected to have a longer working life.

Above left: Guy offered a quality 5/6-ton tipper in the form of their 'Otter'. It had a choice of 4-cyl petrol, or diesel. From 1952 the Perkins P6 was also available. This is a 1952 Holmes cabbed, Gardner 4LK powered Otter with Eaton 2-speed axle as run by Harrison's Limeworks, Penrith. It has lost its famous Indian's head motif.

Above: Earliest full-forward control models from Morris Commercial were the 'FVs'. They had a 3.7 litre 4-cyl petrol or Saurer designed 4.45 litre 6-cyl diesel. Rear-hinged doors were known as 'suicide' doors as they flew open if not properly latched. This is a 1950 5 cu.yd tipper with standard body.

Left: Rowe-Hillmaster tippers were built at Liskeard, Cornwall. Engines were available from Gardner, Meadows and Leyland or AEC. This one dates from 1959.

Road Services (Forth) Ltd and its associate Company, Road Services (Caledonian) Ltd were formed following de-nationalisation in 1955. They operated a nationwide transport service, initially with ex-BRS vehicles which were soon replaced by new lorries like this Leyland Beaver. It was registered in 1955 and is seen here in Dunstable, complete with 8-ton drawbar trailer. It is in Forth's old livery of two-tone green with red wheels and chassis and black wings. Leyland Beavers were rated at 12 tons gvw when solo and at 24 tons gtw with a trailer. They were powered by the 'O.600' 9.8 litre 6-cylinder oil engine.

Above, left to right:
Drawbar trailers were popular in the fifties in spite of the legal requirement to carry a second man whose job it was to operate the trailer brake lever and to generally assist the driver when manoeuvring, hitching or un-hitching the trailer. Generally 4-wheeled trailer models were powered by larger engines as was this 1953 Mandator with its 9.6 litre unit developing 125bhp. Scott's of Oldham ran it, mainly on the distribution of glass containers.

For the movement of goods over short distances ballasted drawbar tractors and independent 4-wheel trailers offered certain advantages, plus an extra measure of flexibility in operation. They were also very manoeuvrable. This is a 1946 Foden DG in the fleet of R Cornell Ltd of London. It was used in and around the Docks.

This S20-cabbed Foden trailer model photographed near Cardiff Docks in June 1957, when only 7 months old, was designed for the new 14 ton gvw limit announced in 1955. GTW was 24 tons. It bears a 1956 Cumberland registration number TAO 34 and is finished in the two tone green livery of London and Welsh Transport.

Left: Yet another Leyland outfit. This time a true classic in the form of a 1954 12.B/1 Beaver with O.600 engine which belonged to the Liverpool based Bents Brewery Company and was used on pub delivery work.

Liverpool hauliers George Davies operated this Gardner powered Atkinson 4-wheeler and trailer in and around the Mersey Docks. It dates from 1955.

One of the Austin '503' tractor and trailer outfits employed by BRS Meat Haulage to transport imported meat from the docks to Smithfield market. It dates from 1957.

Rarely seen away from the dock area this tractor and trailer combination is another example similar to that of BRS Meat Haulage. In this instance the load is bagged feed from Bibby's Mill in Liverpool and the tractor is a 1949 ERF. Bibby's had a number of these outfits and other operators in Liverpool were Jarvis Robinson Transport and the Union Cartage Company.

British Railways had an extensive fleet of road vehicles, though relatively few Leylands. This London based 1956 Beaver and trailer was photographed along Warwick Road carrying four old fashioned lift-off BR containers.

1947 Maudslay Mogul and trailer in use with C & W.H. Taylor. It is seen along the Chaloner Street section of Liverpool's Dock Road. Moguls were powered by the AEC 7.7 litre engine of 95bhp. A David Brown O45 overdrive 5-speed crash box was fitted and a plate on the dash advised drivers not to use overdrive when fully laden and drawing a trailer.

Less common among trailer outfits is this Leyland Comet hauled combination from Warwicks and Richardsons Brewery in Nottingham. A 1955 model, it is seen on the southbound carriageway of the A1. Gross train weight was 17¾ tons.

ARTICS

Articulated vehicles play such a major role in present day haulage, it is difficult to believe that in forties and fifties Britain they took second place to rigids.

The principles of articulation go back to the earliest days of motor vehicles. Thornycroft built a steam powered artic as long ago as 1898. For that matter the heavy horse drawn 4-wheel wagon also took the form of an artic.

Pioneers of articulation in the U.K. were Scammell whose early 10-tonner in 1922 boasted a payload only previously possible on a rigid and trailer. Scammell's domination of the artic business continued into the post-war years with their famous bonneted 'Artic Eight' machines which enjoyed great popularity on both bulk liquid operation and long distance haulage.

In the forties and fifties most artics were employed on low-loader work or for light urban distribution where the flexibility of automatic coupling trailers aided efficiency. This concept was also developed by Scammell in the form of their 'Mechanical Horse' and 'Scarab'.

In the maximum capacity class, artics had no great advantage over rigids, both being limited to 22 tons. In 1955 this limit was raised for both, to 24 tons, when artics were also allowed a 35ft length limit, as opposed to 33ft.

Most lightweight tractors, designed for the 8 ton payload class of artic, were of normal control layout, adapted from short wheelbase tipper chassis, like the Bedford OST, the Austin K4 or the Commer Superpoise. Heavier tractor units were simply shorter versions of two-axle 12-ton gross chassis like the Leyland Beaver, Atkinson T746 and the Maudslay Maharanee.

Artics or 'bendy motors' as they were nick-named, required new driving techniques, which rigid men had to learn, and the trickiest manoeuvre of all was reversing. Those who mastered it, soon discovered that artics were far more manoeuvrable than rigids.

The archetypal 'Articulated Eight' from Scammell. United Diaries were among the leading users of these famous machines which were widely employed on the haulage of bulk liquids in the forties and fifties. Powered by the 102bhp Gardner 6LW with Scammell's own indestructible epicyclic double-reduction rear axle and 6-speed constant mesh gearbox, this model dates from 1946. The design remained virtually unaltered between the mid-thirties and the mid-fifties.

This general view of a BRS depot features a variety of AECs, including two artics. In the right foreground is a Mercury for 18 tons gcw, while to the left and slightly farther back is the heavier 24 ton gcw Mandator.

Albion's offering in the medium weight artic class was the FT111TR, seen here in operation with Girling, the brake equipment manufacturers from Birmingham and Cwmbran. Based on the Chieftain, the FT111TR grossed at 14 tons and had the 4.9 litre 4-cylinder Albion diesel.

This Atkinson T746, photographed with its load of fruit at the side of the old A5 in Dunstable, was one of a number purchased by Alfred Dexter Ltd in 1956. It has a Gardner 6LW and the semi-trailer is a 25ft Dyson. Dexter's were among the earlier long distance hauliers to move over to articulation.

Designated an 8-tonner, the Bedford OSS tractor was usually equipped with Scammell automatic coupling gear (the second 'S' in the model type meant Scammell). It could work in conjunction with Scammell's 3-wheeled Mechanical Horse, which was not intended for long distances. Before regulations called for secondary trailer braking, drivers of automatic coupling artics could couple and un-couple without leaving their cabs.

Higher up the weight range, Bedford offered their diesel powered 'SA' model for payloads of around 10 tons. They were put to hauling more demanding payloads on long distance work by some operators. The tractor wheelbase was only 7ft 2in. This one is a late model dating from 1959 and is coupled to a Carrimore semi-trailer.

Having begun in 1952 with rigid 8-wheelers, Bristol's BRS production was switched to tractor units in 1955 when the trends towards articulation were becoming more evident. This is a 1959 Leyland engined HA6L coupled to a Bristol ST semi-trailer.

Although taken in the mid sixties, as is evident from the post BTC fleet number, this striking colour shot in Liverpool docks could easily date from the fifties. The Bristol HA6LL is waiting on Regent Road. These vehicles were developed as the standard 'max-cap' outfit for use by British Road Services. At 24tons gcw their future was bleak when the new 32ton weight limit was introduced in 1964.

For short haul operations at 12 tons gross, the bonneted Dennis Horla was a quality engineered rival to the mass-produced light tractors. It was purpose-designed for use with automatic coupling type semi-trailers. They were built at Guildford between 1946 and 1962. This one belonged to the Co-operative Wholesale Society and dates from 1946. Originally Horlas had the 3.7 litre 67bhp 4-cylinder side valve petrol engine, but later models, from 1953 onwards, had the option of a Perkins P6.

Dating from 1947 this ERF CI6.4 tractor was one of a fleet of ERFs used by Liverpool-based Criddle and Co Ltd to distribute animal feed. They operated over a wide area, including Central Wales, where this photograph was taken. The trailer is of the 'four-in-line' type.

Heavy duties required solidly built machines like this 1948 ERF operated by Lund of Otley in Yorkshire. H. Lund Ltd of Gay Lane, Otley also specialised in the movement of long loads. This ERF tractor bears a 1948 registration number and was 20 years old when photographed.

BRS used a wide variety of makes and types of tractor unit. Though outnumbered by Leylands, AECs and Seddons, Guys like this 'Otter' of 1953 were used on medium duty operations. With a gcw of 15 tons the Otter carried a legal 10 ton payload and was powered by a Perkins P6 diesel. It has the Motor Panels. pattern cab, similar to that used by Thornycroft. Some of the Guy cabs were built by Willenhall.

The Leyland '600' series was conceived and grew up in the days of rigids. Beaver tractors were in the minority. They were 'max-cap' artics in their day, designed for the top gcw of 24 tons when used with a tandem or 'four-in-line' type semi-trailer. Photographed in Luton this 4000 gallon tank outfit was registered in 1957 and was used by Cleveland Petroleum for garage deliveries.

For use with either automatic or fifth wheel coupling trailers, the bonneted Leyland Comet 90 tractor unit was a popular and versatile machine for gross weights up to 17.85 tons gcw, giving a payload of around 12tons. They were built up to 1959, the last ones having the 100hp 'O.351' engine. This is a 1952 outfit operated by London hauliers S. A. Hartz Ltd.

With its twin oscillating axle semi trailer and larger than standard fuel tank, this Leyland Comet ECOS2.6R looks every inch a British haulage vehicle of the late fifties. It belonged to the well-known Enfield based company, L. T. Redburn Ltd.

Included in this late fifties shot of BRS Kingsway depot in Luton are two forward control Leyland Comet artics, and a Vulcan 6PF artic as well as three Holmes cabbed Austin '503' 4-wheelers.

As an urban, short-haul artic the Scammell Scarab was unrivalled. Extremely manoeuvrable, it could be rated at 3 tons or 6 tons and was a worthy successor to the famous Mechanical Horse. Hundreds of Scarabs were employed on local deliveries by British Railways.

An ex-Army Thornycroft Nubian put to use as an artic for round timber by Ivor Read, Mitcheldean, photographed passing through the Forest of Dean on the A4136.

Scammell were the unassailed leaders of articulation in the pre-war and early post-war days. Long before the industry became gripped by the idea of artics as serious rivals to rigids, Scammells like this 1947 'Eight Wheeler' van, were earning their keep on long distance work with large operators such as General Roadways and Edward Box. Scammells built tractor and trailer (or motive unit and carrier, as they preferred to call them) as a matched combination, and had their own patent 'ball and socket' coupling, which was not of the quick release type. For most of the time it was left coupled-up. This Tate & Lyle example, featuring a traditional looking 'bow-fronted' trailer, is an exception to the rule, having conventional trailer support legs.

SIX
WHEELERS

Until the arrival of the first rigid eight-wheeler* in 1929, the rigid six was the largest of lorries. The origins of the rigid six-wheeler go back to the turn of the century, but the first significant British examples appeared in the late twenties when Foden, Sentinel and Atkinson built their 12 ton payload 6-wheeled 'steamers'. They offered an attractive alternative to the four-wheeler and trailer which had the additional disadvantage of a lower speed limit.

When the 1930 Road Traffic Act laid down clearly defined weight limits, three axled vehicles were specified as having a 19 ton gross weight.

Most leading heavy vehicle manufacturers soon introduced petrol and diesel powered models to take 12 ton payloads.

In addition to the maximum weight six-wheelers there were numerous conversions carried out on light four-wheelers. Adding a 'third axle' provided about 50% more payload capacity and specialist conversions were offered by firms like Boys, Carrimore, Unipower and the well known Primrose and York.

Another breed of six-wheeler born in the thirties, was the twin-steer, or 'Chinese six', pioneered by ERF in association with haulage contractors E. B. Ward of Warrington. Although the twin-steer concept had been toyed with in the early part of the century ERF's CI5.6TS was the first true production 'Chinese six'. Grossing at 15 tons it carried 30% more than a four-wheeler and when carriers' licencing was by unladen weight a 'Chinese six' could legitimately be 'slipped' into the fleet without applying for an increase on the licence because it was only a ton or so heavier than a four-wheeler. Used with a trailer it could handle 17 ton payloads and the second steer provided an additional margin of safety from front wheel blow-outs.

* Sentinel 'DG8' steamer

A veteran in maturity. Dating from 1949 this AEC Mammoth Major Mk III 6-wheeler is typical of long distance haulage lorries built to withstand the pressures of sustained nationwide tramping. It was 21 years old when photographed at Kennington, London. During its life it had been re-cabbed, using an adaptation of the Mk V cab and an extra fuel tank has been fitted to double its capacity to 80 gallons.

Right: Featuring a more common pattern of cab, this 1952 '3671' AEC Mk III Mammoth Major 6, was photographed at Bradford. It belonged to wool importers Sanderson, Murray & Elder. AEC were among the leading producers of heavy-duty rigid 6-wheelers in the fifties. In essence they were exactly the same as the 8-wheelers, but less the second steering axle. Hence they had ample reserves of strength and power to cope with their allotted 12-ton payloads.

Left to right:
Another classic Mammoth Major 6, this time from the well known fleet of Starch Products, of Slough.

Ex-RAF Austin K6 '6x4' trucks were a common sight in the post-war years. They were only a lightweight machine with a 3-ton payload rating (on military service – 5/6 ton civilian) This one was photographed in Newark, about to be overtaken by a '152 Omnivan' (J2's predecessor), from the same manufacturer.

This Atkinson M1266 tipper belonging to Nottinghamshire based hauliers, Bexon Brothers, has had an extra badge superimposed on the radiator. It dates from 1946 and is fitted with a typical high-sided body for bulk coke.

Formerly run by Stanworth's Transport (Burnley) Ltd, this Atkinson L1266 was one of a 15-strong fleet merged into William Nuttall & Sons of Clifton, Manchester. Stanworths' splendid grey and red livery with gold signwriting was retained. The message on the cab side proclaimed simply 'London and the North'. It had a Gardner 6LW under the bonnet, which powered most post-war Atkinsons. Stanworth's operated nightly trunk services to Glasgow, Newcastle and London.

To gain more payload, many operators had 4-wheelers converted to 6-wheelers. This 1959 'S' type bulker is one such example, operated by Tunnel Refineries of Greenwich. The gvw would have been raised from the standard 10.75 tons to 15.46 for roughly a ton more on the tare weight. Best known conversion specialists were Primrose, York and Boys.

This is the 'Jubilant' 6-wheeler from Dennis Brothers of Guildford. Introduced in 1946 the Jubilant was rated at the full legal 19 tons gross, and was powered by a 7.5 litre 6-cylinder diesel. It was Dennis's largest vehicle, although a handful of 8-wheeled Jubilants were built in the early sixties.

With its trusty '6LW' the ERF 6.6 upheld ERF's reputation for solid reliability. It adhered to the David Brown gearbox and Kirkstall axle recipe by which ERF stood firm in the fifties. Continuous flow hydraulic wedge brakes left something to be desired, especially at low speeds when the servo was least effective. This 1950 model worked in the Union Cartage fleet.

This ERF CI6.6 dates from 1947 and has the more proven vacuum hydraulic braking system with cam expanders. In other respects it is similar, mechanically, to the 6.6 at the foot of page 74.

Many ex-Ministry Foden DG 6-wheelers found their way into transport fleets in the fifties. This is a typical example, one of a number operated on timber haulage by Arnold Laver & Co. of Sheffield.

When Albion first introduced their lightweight rigid six it was called a 'Chieftain 6-wheeler'. It was later re-named 'Reiver', a name which the Leyland group continued to use until the last 'G' cabbed 6-wheelers were built in 1980. This earlier example dates from 1958. These had a choice of diesel engines – the FT107 model had the Albion EN287 4-cylinder and the PF107 had the Leyland O.351 'Comet' 6-cylinder.

This impressive ERF 'Chinese' 6-wheeler is referred to in the cover caption on page 2. It is vividly reminiscent of fifties haulage when Liverpool Docks were bustling with activity.

A Foden DG tipper which originally started life as a 4-wheeler, only to be converted later into this single drive 6-wheeler. The original model actually dates from pre-war days. It was used by a brick manufacturer in the Manchester area.

A 'V' front S18 cab graces this Foden FG6/12 flat, operated by Andrew Wishart & Sons of Dysart near Kirkcaldy. Wishart's fleet is noted for its superb signwriting in the traditional Scottish style. This FG was registered in 1953.

Dating from 1957, this S18 cabbed FG6/12 was operated by Scottish haulier W. F. Wight Ltd who belonged to the large Halifax-based Holdsworth Group.

Foden's frequent developments in cab designs yielded many appearance changes in the forties and fifties. In 1956 this smart 'S20' version came in to replace the S18 'V' front. This vehicle was engaged on general haulage with A. M. Walker of Cosby, Leicester.

While Leyland Comet tippers were common, 3-axled versions certainly were not. This large capacity bulker appears to have a third axle conversion which would have increased its recommended payload from 7 tons to around 11. The O.351 diesel was well able to pull that weight. The vehicle dates from 1955.

Leyland's off-the-shelf rigid 6-wheeler was the Hippo, powered by the 9.8 litre O.600 engine. They flew the flag for British quality engineering in the export-conscious fifties. Along with the Beaver, Octopus and Steer of the same family, they were popular with large own-account fleets where a heavy lorry was sometimes expected to give up to 15 or 20 years service. Charles Brown belonged to Spillers, and this Hippo dates from 1949.

Spillers, the flour millers, ran a variety of Leyland heavies, like this 19.H/7 Hippo dating from 1953. Their large fleet was based at Silvertown, and also featured Octopus 8-wheelers and several 4 and 8-wheelers from the Albion stable. This Hippo is built on the longest wheelbase to take three 'hopper' style tanks with blower equipment. The vehicle is fitted out to operate with a drawbar trailer.

Among the less common 6-wheelers were Maudslay Mustangs. These twin-steers were powered by the AEC 7.7 litre diesel. This particular example was in the fleet of Marley Tiles during the fifties, and was based at Leighton Buzzard. It dates from 1948.

This 1958 Seddon Mk14 trailing axle 6-wheeler, with Gardner engine, belonged to J.H. Henderson & Sons of Alston, Cumbria and was photographed along Chaloner Street in Liverpool Docks. Along with many rigids of its era, it fell victim to the artic uprising of the sixties, when it was cut down into a 4-wheel tractor unit. Legend has it that it ended its days in an accident, when it came to grief on Strawberry Bank, Shap Fell.

NUN 413 was a Sentinel 6-cylindered DV66M medium 6-wheeler, having the benefit of greater power than the 4/6DV (below). It was fitted with the 123bhp direct injection engine. This photograph was taken in July 1958, co-inciding with the end of its working career with Dee Valley Transport, who owned it from new. It was Dee Valley's policy to name all their lorries and their fleet was always well turned out. This vehicle was named 'The Lily of the Valley', the valley being the Vale of Langollen. It spent much of its working life carrying dairy products and margarine.

An early example of Sentinel's 4/6DV light 6-wheeler, which was spawned from the original 4/4DV 4-wheeler. It was the product of a joint development between Sentinel's engineers, and Tom Ward, Managing Director of Sentinel's main agents, North Cheshire Motors. Powered by the small 90bhp 4-cylinder diesel, 4/6DVs were very light and economical to operate. GUJ 652 was built as a works demonstrator, later passing to Beresford's Transport of Tunstall in whose livery it appears here. The photograph was taken on the forecourt of the old Three Sisters Cafe on the A5 near Markyate, and the Sentinel, still fitted with its works dropside body, is loaded with grinding pebbles for the Potteries.

'Mustang' was originally used by Maudslay for their Chinese six, but when Maudslay was dropped from the ACV range AEC used the name for its own Mercury based twin-steer model which, along with Mercurys, were built at the Maudslay works. This 1959 example is from the well known fleet of Richardson's (Hull) Transport Co., the trading name of Pickering Road Haulage Ltd.

Seen taking part at the Lorry Driver of the Year finals, this 1954 ERF 5.6TS has the classic Jennings 'Streamline' coach-built cab. It was finished in the smart yellow and red livery of Kenneth Wilson, the Leeds based corn merchants.

This side-view shot emphasises the critical axle spacing on Chinese sixes. The rear axle takes approximately half the gross load and is set well back in order to transfer more weight onto the front. While the type was popular for trailer work, the short rear overhang and heavy steering made reversing manoeuvres difficult.

This fine 15.S/1 Leyland Steer ran in the fleet of Kiveton Park Steel & Wire Works, near Sheffield. It dates from 1949 and has the O.600 engine. It appears to have been re-cabbed with the later '600' series steel cab.

Six wheelers and trailers were always a popular combination. Running solo a 6-wheeler grossed at 19 tons and carried approximately 12. A trailer increased the legal gross weight to 32 tons, making it a profitable outfit. In most respects the leading heavy 6-wheelers of the era are identical with their 8-wheeled brethren, but less the second steering axle. This ERF 6.6 dates from 1952 and was photographed in Liverpool Docks.

Top left: A 1951 AEC Mammoth Major Mk III 6-wheeler, with 4-wheel drawbar trailer, seen at the Manningham Lane depot of Henry Long, Bradford. Much of Henry Long's traffic consisted of wool between the Docks and the Bradford mills.

Top right: This Atkinson M1266 with Gardner 6LW is a 1952 model and it worked for the Stanton and Staveley Chemical Company. Note the 10.50x20 front tyres, while the rear axles have 40x8 duals. This arrangement gave more load capacity to the front axle.

Right: Another trailer outfit – this time a 1951 Leyland, in operation with Walter Southworth of Rufford near Ormskirk, Lancs. It bears a Beaver radiator badge and therefore may have been converted from a 4-wheeler, in order to gain more payload.

EIGHT WHEELERS

Throughout the forties and fifties the rigid eight was Britain's top-of-the-range long distance haulage vehicle. Its origins lay in the early thirties when 22 tons was allowed on vehicles with 'more than 3 axles'.

Having an 8-wheeler in their range marked a manufacturer as a true heavy vehicle builder. While most mass-producers offered 6-wheeled adaptations of their basic four-wheelers, only the recognised quality-built ranges from AEC, Leyland, ERF and so on included rigid eights.

Originally rigid eights were not permitted to draw a trailer – a regulation which was relaxed in 1942 under war-time pressures for maximum efficiency. This also enabled the pulling of a trailer-mounted gas producer when fuel was in short supply. There were nine makes of rigid eight-wheeler in Britain in the immediate post-war period and, during the fifties, four more were added, namely Bristol, Guy, Seddon Diesel and TVW. Dennis from Guildford built a very small number and Rutland also listed a rigid eight in their 1957 model list, though there is no evidence that any entered service in the U.K.

The role of the rigid eight in the forties and fifties was far reaching. They were the flagships of the leading long distance trunk hauliers. They served an important role in the growth of bulk haulage of liquids and powders. In tipping and construction work they came into their own, having good traction and superior stability.

While many countries world-wide saw an increase in the use of rigid eight-wheelers during the seventies and eighties, Britain has, for five decades, been the centre of the eight-wheeler world.

If one type of rigid 8-wheeler epitomised the fifties scene, it was the Leyland 22.O/1 Octopus. It typified the well engineered products which earned Leyland a good reputation at home and abroad. Leylands were built entirely from their own components, even down to the plain, but functional driver's cab. This is an early example registered in 1948.

A 1953 AEC 3871 Mammoth Major Mk III, trailing-axle 8-wheeler in Whitbread's livery, on contract from BRS. It has a Park Royal Vehicles style of coachbuilt cab and the 9.6 litre 6-cylinder oil engine. Air pressure brakes operated on the first, third and fourth axles.

Pulled up alongside the old A5 at Dunstable in the late fifties are two of Bowaters' well known fleet of AEC Mk III 8-wheelers.

Top: This 1953 AEC Mammoth Major Mk III from BRS Swansea, was photographed prior to the introduction of the new style BTC roundel.

Centre: Another Mk III of the same year from Kings Lynn branch bears the new badge. This angle emphasises the AEC's long wheelbase of 18ft 9½ ins. In Britain they were rated at 22 tons but for overseas they grossed 25 tons when fitted with 10.00x20 tyres.

Lower: Two of the most common BRS 'rigid eights' of the fifties – the AEC Mk III and the Leyland Octopus, in this case an air-braked 24.O/4. The AEC is JCY 646 (1G355) from Cardiff and the Octopus LDM 275 (1C330) from Queensferry. Both are loaded with steel.

One of the larger AEC fleets was that of the Marston Valley Brick Company from Ridgmont near Bedford. This Mk III dates from 1954 and features the Duramin light alloy cab which both Marston Valley and the London Brick Company used widely.

This colour shot, taken in the late fifties, shows one of the well known Guinness Albion CX7N tankers which were based at Park Royal in West London. They had 75 barrel (2700 gallon) tanks from Thompsons or Butterfields. This one was new in 1950 and has the more common Thompson tank.

A 1948 Atkinson L1586 of Entress Transport, Gorseinon, near Swansea. This was 18 years old when photographed, and although showing signs of wear, was still in regular use. Such a long working life, on intensive long distance haulage speaks volumes for the quality of Atkinson products. L1586 models featured the 6LW/David Brown/Kirkstall formula of the forties and fifties.

This ERF 6.8 is a 1951 model. This, and the Atkinson shown above, had similar specifications, featuring the Gardner 6LW 8.4 litre engine with 112bhp, the David Brown DB557 direct-top 5-speed gearbox with constant-mesh and Kirkstall overhead-worm rear axles. This specification package was as common as the Cummins, Fuller and Rockwell formula of the eighties.

16 tons of sheet steel is the load for this 1950 Mk III 8-wheeler of D. David & Sons, Bridgend, seen waiting to unload at Luton in 1958. Wartime camouflage is still visible on the factory wall. The AEC Mammoth Major stands out as Britain's most successful and enduring breed of eight-wheeler. The very first internal combustion engined rigid eight to be marketed, in 1934, it retained its basic external appearance for over two decades. The original '680' model gave way to the '386' Mark II in 1936; the '3871' Mark III appeared in 1948 and the 'G8RA' Mark V in 1958. Spanning well over 40 years, 'Mammoth Major' was one of the longest running model names. It finally disappeared with the last '3TG8R' Ergomatic 30 ton gvw models in 1978.

Below: For tipper work AEC offered the 14ft 6½in wheelbase chassis, like this one from the fleet of Southern Contractors of Sevenoaks in Kent.

Left: Popularly nick-named the 'tin-front' this type of AEC Mammoth Major was virtually the same specification as those with exposed radiators, but its wide dummy radiator gave it a more modern appearance and many had the 11.3 litre engine giving 150bhp. Hanson is one of the greatest names in British road haulage and their red lorries were a familiar sight along the Yorkshire to London trunk route. FHG 772, a 1957 model, had the old-style van body with open roof, for top-loading with woollen bales. A tarpaulin sheet protected the load from the weather.

Right: B. R. Mills of Chesterfield were well known for their fine fleet of Albion CX7 8-wheelers, many of which had large capacity van bodies. This example dates from 1948.

Like most heavy vehicle builders of the period, Albion built the chassis and scuttle to take a variety of bespoke cabs. This HD57 of Bulwark Transport, Chippenham, KWV 454, had a Duramin light alloy version. It was on contract to Stevens & Hynson of Barking and was photographed on the A40 near London in 1956.

Taken in Liverpool this shot of a 1949 Albion CX7N in the livery of A & A Peate of Oswestry emphasises the distinctive, if somewhat dated, appearance of post-war Albions. It started life with J. N. Miller of Wolverhampton. Albion CX7N models had brakes on the second, third and fourth axles. Power unit was the Albion EN243 6-cylinder diesel. They had a '2-stick' transmission with 4-speed main and 2-speed auxiliary box.

This Atkinson L1586 bulk grain carrier dates from 1951, and features the period style coachbuilt cab which hardly differed from the original pre-war version.

This late fifties shot shows an S1586 Atkinson flat in the old green and red colours of Richard Thomas and Baldwins. A number of South Wales operators used similar short wheelbase flats to carry steel. They were built on the tipper wheelbase of 15ft 1½ins.

London-based long distance hauliers Cyprien Fox Ltd had a fine fleet of dark blue 8-wheelers. This Atkinson L1786 was a year old when photographed in Luton in 1958.

A classic from the days when BRS were adding large numbers of 'rigid eights' to their ranks. This Willenhall cabbed ERF 6.8 was a typical maximum capacity rigid of which there were many based at depots in the East Anglia region, including Ipswich, Peterborough, and Whittlesey.

In its striking livery of pale yellow with red writing this 1947 Foden DG6/15 tanker operated in the fleet of Monsanto Chemicals from Ruabon in North Wales. Power unit was the Gardner 6LW and it is shod, like most DGs, on 40 x 8 tyres.

This ERF 6.8 dates from 1947 and has a Butterfield 3500 gallon oil tank body. Reliance Transport took delivery of the very first ERF 'rigid eight' tanker in 1934.

Perhaps the most striking of fifties cab designs was the 'KV' introduced by ERF in 1954. This 1955 eight wheeled flat of J. M. Watkins was photographed in Luton in 1958.

Connoisseurs of the 'rigid eight' could wish for no better a specimen than this Gardner 6LW powered short wheelbase Foden FG6/15 from the Tate & Lyle fleet. Photographed at the Silvertown Refinery it was one of a large number of similar machines, designed for the bulk movement of refined granulated sugar. They operated between the refinery and packing stations or large customers, such as confectionery and biscuit manufacturers. The distinctive tank bodies were built by the Airscrew Company & Jicwood using double skinned insulated construction on a hardwood frame. Loading was carried out with the tank tipped to 45 degrees, the sugar entering through the large central filler neck. The small neck was a vent. Discharge was by gravity on the earlier tanks but later ones were equipped with blowers.

In contrast with the 1953 Foden below, this 1950 model has the original 'flat front' S18 cab. W. T. Flather of Sheffield operated a number of FG6/15s, many of which originated with the Cement Marketing Company.

A standard V-front S18 'Saloon' cab graces this 1953 FG6/15 photographed in 1958. Note the semaphore trafficators and small driving mirror – reminders of the pre-motorway era.

Laporte's Fullers Earth plant at Redhill is the setting for this shot depicting a 1953 Foden FG6/15 alongside a 1955 BRS Bristol from Guildford branch. The Foden has a Duramin cab while the Bristol has one of BBW (Bristol Body Works) manufacture.

This mid-fifties shot taken at Dunstable, shows one of the original Willenhall cabbed Guy Invincibles from 1955. They were based on the AEC Mammoth Major Mark III chassis but with a choice of Gardner 6LW or Meadows 6DC engine with David Brown gearbox. The Guy chassis frame was bolted, while the AEC frame was riveted. In most other respects they were identical.

Another early style Invincible, this time a 1957 tanker from the Hackney-based fleet of Carless, Capel & Leonard. It carried solvents.

After four years production of the AEC based Invincible, Guy Motors hit the headlines in 1958 with this striking new model, featuring an ultra-modern cab with four headlamps and a large 'wrap round' windscreen. They caused quite a sensation at the Earls Court Show of that year and their individualistic appearance made them a classic of their era. They were offered in two wheelbases of 13ft 9ins for tipper work and 17ft 9ins as shown here. 5764 WE was brand new when photographed in Luton and was one of the first of the new Invincibles to enter service. Riley's operated a regular Sheffield to Luton service, bringing steel forgings for the motor industry.

Above: Well known operator Richard Biffa ran a number of
Leyland Octopus and Hippo tippers. This Octopus from 1954
was employed for a time on the construction of Britain's first
M1 motorway section between Watford and Crick. It had the
trusty O.600 oil engine.

One of the celebrated Octopus fleets was that of Sealand
District Transport, an own-account subsidiary of John
Summers Steel from Shotton. These tastefully liveried
22.O/1 dropside 8-wheelers on 40x8 tyres, were a common
sight throughout the fifties. This shot, taken in 1958, shows
a 1953 model with vacuum hydraulic brakes.

Left: The Leyland Octopus 22.O/1 was one of the most popular and successful maximum weight rigids of all time. Large numbers went to BRS in the fifties but many went to other operators like Monmouthshire Transport who were a subsidiary of the Steel Company of Wales. This late fifties photograph taken at Luton depicts three 22.O/1s, loaded with baled scrap steel, awaiting the night men to take them back to South Wales.

Right: This 24.O/4 air-braked Octopus with the later style of 600 series steel cab was less than a year old when photographed along Cowbridge Road, Cardiff in 1956. It is in the grey and green livery of Jones Motors, Kenfig Hill, near Bridgend.

A 1952 Leyland 22.O/1 Octopus 3600 gallon petrol tanker captured on colour film in London in the early 'sixties.

A 1954 24.O/4 air-braked Octopus from BRS Queensferry still carries its BTC 'lion and wheel' badge, set in the circle of sea-green, the North Western Divisional colour. The photograph was actually taken in 1966.

Rare indeed is this Maudslay 8-wheeler, apparently dating from the early forties. At first sight it appears to be a Mikado model, but the name 'Maharajah' on the radiator suggests that Annis & Company may have converted it from a 6-wheeler. The early forties Maudslay heavies were Gardner powered.

An AEC 9.6 litre diesel engined Maudslay Meritor operating with William Harper of Liverpool. It dates from 1949 and was chassis number 85163. The majority of Maudslay Meritors were built to the order of British Road Services. The last of 256 Meritors was built at their Parkside Works, Coventry in 1951.

The Scammell 'Rigid Eight' was a very individual machine, quite different from the conventional designs of the period. Originally it featured rubber front suspension with a unique load-equalising balance beam arrangement giving very close axle spacing. The rear bogie was equally unusual as it too had rubber suspension without the usual axle tube for the rearmost wheels. Instead it simply had short stub axles. The driving axle was Scammell's epicyclic double reduction bevel unit. A remote six-speed overdrive gearbox was fitted and eight wheel braking had air/rod operation. Front wheel brakes were air actuated and rear wheel brakes worked through a mechanical linkage with air assistance. Rubber front suspension was switched to coil springs after the first couple of years and later was reworked to suit steel multi-leaf springs. Many post war Rigid Eights had underslung 4-spring rear suspension and some had inverted 2-spring arrangements employing Kirkstall overhead worm double drive bogies. But the early pattern of rear bogie continued to be available, clearly identifiable by the single 'balloon' rear tyres. United Molasses were one of the leading operators of the type and this example was delivered as late as 1958.

OXO 98, a 1953 'Rigid Eight', seen here in Cardiff in 1956, had the alternative type of rear bogie featuring 4-spring steel suspension. In other respects it was similar to the United Molasses example on the previous pages.

Large numbers of the country's Scammell 'Rigid Eights' found their way into the well known fleet of S. Harrison & Sons of Sheffield, who continued to operate them well into the seventies. Here, SML 496, a 1947 model poses in Harrison's Sheffield depot.

One of the best known Scammell 8-wheeler fleets in Scotland was Young's Express Deliveries of Paisley, instantly recognisable by their 'XS' (Paisley) registrations. Also bearing a Paisley registration from 1942, is this 'Rigid Eight' in the dark blue livery of the Clydebank Haulage Company from Roman Bridge, Duntocher. They were part of the Glasgow Hiring Company. XS 5458 has a load of Teacher's Whisky on its way through Glasgow Docks.

This 'Rigid Eight', photographed in its latter years, probably began life in the Guinness fleet. It is a 1950 model and was operating on contract to the Accrington Brick and Tile Company in the late sixties.

British manufacturers were still bringing out new rigid eights in the late fifties but pro artic legislation was only 'around the corner'. In the sixties artic sales overtook those of rigids. Seddon Diesel entered the eight wheeler market for the first time in 1958 and pulled out in 1964. The DD8 was their first offering, seen here in Scarr's of Selby's livery.

Top, Left to Right:
Late-comers to the eight wheeler scene, Seddon's DD8 and SD8 (double and single drive) were designed for 24 ton gvw with a 28 ton gvw potential should proposed legislation take effect allowing 28 ton gvw tankers. That proposal was dropped. This tanker of the Murgatroyd Salt & Chemical Company went on the road in 1959.

A BRS contract vehicle in the colours of the British Sugar Corporation of Kidderminster. This DD8 was photographed at BRS Wellington and has similar tank bodywork to that fitted on Tate & Lyle tankers, one of which is described on page 100.

In its smart red livery with gold writing this Seddon DD8 of Fordhouses Service Station was photographed in Dunstable. It had a Gardner 6LX 150 engine and dates from late 1959.

Right: Thornycroft offered two basic types of eight-wheeler. This is a 1958 PK/QR6 with 'standard' cab. It succeeded the earlier PF/NR6 in 1956. The larger 9.83 litre QR6 engine developed 130bhp, while the earlier NR6 was a 7.88 litre unit, giving only 100bhp. Both had 8-wheel air brakes when the majority of eight-wheelers only had brakes on the first, third and fourth axles.

116

With a Gardner 6LW putting out 112bhp from its 8.4 litres, this superb Atkinson eight-wheeler and trailer outfit from the famous Holt Lane Transport fleet of Prescot, Liverpool, was not not overpowered for its full legal gross weight of 32 tons. The mechanical specification of the Atkinson L1586 did not change significantly in 20 years of production, but during the war some were equipped with AEC 7.7 litre engines when Gardners were in short supply. Certain operators, notably Whitbreads Brewery, ordered the AEC 9.6 engine for their Atkinsons in the fifties. The Gardner 6LX '150' became available in 1958, and prior to that a small number were fitted with the 8LW '150' straight eight. Craddock Brothers from Coven, Staffs operated one such vehicle designated an L1588.

Employed on trunk operations this Harrison's of Dewsbury AEC Mk III was photographed at their London depot in Westbourne Road, N.7. It was once on the fleet of Marston Valley Brick Company. When it finally came out of service with Harrisons it was converted into a recovery vehicle.

Right: Liverpool based haulier Michael McKenna ran a regular trunk service to South Wales. This is one of that Company's maximum capacity trailer outfits hauled by a 1954 AEC Mk III.

Opposite: Photographed in Cardiff in 1956 this new 'tin-front' AEC Mk III and trailer, of Silver Roadways Ltd, is loaded up ready for the London trunk. This superb outfit epitomises the maximum-weight long distance lorries of its era.

Seen against a background of its native dockland this fully laden 24.O/4 Octopus and drawbar trailer belonged to Edward Derbyshire of Liverpool. Liverpool was particularly well endowed with Leyland Octopus trailer outfits. The Octopus breed spanned 44 years, beginning with the TEW8/9 in 1935 and ending with the tilt cab Ergomatic Octopus II in 1979. In between were the TEW11/12, 22.O/1-3, 24.O/4-5, 'LAD' Power Plus and the tilt cab Ergomatic. The O.680 11.1 litre engine appeared in 1958 with 150bhp giving ample performance for heavy trailer work. The 'Power Plus' engines (E600 and P680) in 1960 gave outputs of 140 and 200bhp respectively. The very last 30ton Octopus II had the 11.1 litre TL11A turbo with 290bhp. For subsequent rigid eight wheelers, Leyland adopted the title 'Constructor', aptly named as they were developed by Scammell from the Routeman. Originally 'Constructor' was the title which Scammell gave to its heavy cross-country 6 x 6.

One eight-wheeler seen from another. This photograph was taken from the cab of an AEC 8-wheeler and shows a 1952 Atkinson L1586 and trailer in the livery of Thames Board Mills of Warrington on the A5117 Ellsmere Port to Runcorn road.

With their Leyland O.600 engines, Bristol HG6L 8-wheelers were well suited to operate with drawbar trailers. They had full air-brakes. This Birmingham based trailer outfit is an early example, dating from 1953 and features a Burlingham cab.

Perhaps the largest users of the early fifties Leyland Octopus were BRS. They were based all over the country with the main concentrations in the South Wales area. This shot shows a 1954 22.O/1 from Central Liverpool hauling a wool-laden trailer up the steady bank on the A650 out of Bradford.

A picture to sum up the twilight years of old style British haulage. The late '59 24.O/4 Octopus and trailer with its neatly sheeted load is a good example from the pre-artic, pre-motorway days. The whole transport scene underwent sweeping changes in the sixties and this type of outfit did not belong in the new fast-moving motorway era. At 7ft 6in wide it did not take standard size pallets. With a 24ft long body it could not cope with long 'ISO' containers. At 34 mph it could not achieve motorway speeds. With its multi-pull ratchet handbrake it could not meet C & U regulations. In its day it gave stalwart service, but it was overtaken by progress.

MANUFACTURERS'
A to Z

This section is intended as a brief guide to British manufacturers who were active during the forties and fifties. The product information is no more than a broad summary and relates to U.K. civilian on-road goods vehicles within the period and scope of this book. The author cannot be held responsible for errors and omissions.

Abbreviations: w. – Wheel, N/C – Normal Control, F/C – Forward Control

Manufacturers photographs

AEC Southall, Middx. (1912–1979) Heavy duty 4, 6 & 8 w. F/C diesel. Formed ACV with Maudslay in 1948. Crossley joined ACV in 1951. ACV merged with Leyland in 1962.

ALBION Scotstoun, Glasgow (1902–1972) Medium duty 4 w. F/C petrol & diesel. Heavy duty 4, 6 & 8 w. F/C diesel. Taken over by Leyland in 1951.

ATKINSON Preston, Lancs. (1916–1975) Medium duty 4 w. F/C diesel. Heavy duty 4, 6 & 8 w. F/C diesel. Taken over by Seddon Diesel Vehicles 1970.

AUSTIN Longbridge, Birmingham (1908–1968) Bathgate, East Lothian (1961–1968) Light and medium duty 4w. N/C & F/C petrol and diesel. Formed BMC with Morris 1952. BMC merged with Leyland 1968.

Early fifties Austin 'Loadstar' Series 2.

BEDFORD (Vauxhall Motors Ltd), Luton, Beds (1931–1987). Light and medium duty 4 w. N/C & F/C petrol and diesel. Owned by General Motors Corporation. Sold to AWD 1987.

BMC See Austin & Morris Commercial.

BRISTOL Brislington, Bristol (1908–1964) Heavy duty F/C diesel rigid 8 wheelers & artics (1952–1964) Nationalised 1948 and built vehicles solely for BRS.

COMMER Luton, Beds (1905–1976) Light & medium duty 4 w. N/C & F/C petrol and diesel. Joined Rootes Group 1928. Acquired by Chrysler 1973.

1946 Dodge 'Major' 6-tonner.

CROSSLEY Errwood Park, Stockport (1912–1956). AECs were marketed as Crossley in certain countries following ACV's takeover in 1951.

DENNIS Guildford, Surrey (1904–to date) Light, medium & heavy duty 4 & 6 w. N/C & F/C petrol and diesel. Small number of 8 wheelers built 1961. Became Hestair Dennis 1977.

DODGE Kew, Surrey (1933–1967) Dunstable, Beds (1967–1987). Light & medium duty 4 w. N/C & F/C petrol and diesel. Owned by Chrysler Corporation. Acquired by Peugeot-Citroen 1978. Renamed Renault Truck Industries 1984.

ERF Sandbach, Cheshire (1933–to date) Medium & heavy duty 4, 6 (F/C & semi-F/C) & 8 w. (F/C) diesel. 88R petrol engined 8 w. in 1962.

FODEN Sandbach, Cheshire (1902 to date – origins 1856). Medium & heavy duty 4 and heavy duty 6 & 8 w. F/C diesel. Famous steam engine and wagon builders 1880–1934. Taken over by Paccar Corporation in 1980.

FORD Trafford Park, Manchester/Dagenham, Essex (1915–1986). Light & medium duty 4 & 6 w. N/C & F/C petrol and diesel. Products sold as Fordson, Fordson Thames and Ford Thames between 1933 and 1965. Became part of IVECO in 1986.

GUY Wolverhampton, Staffs (1914–1980) Light, medium & heavy duty 4-w. N/C & F/C petrol and diesel, heavy duty 6 & 8 w. F/C diesel. Acquired by Jaguar 1961. Merged with BMC 1964 and then into British Leyland 1968.

JENSEN West Bromwich, Staffs (1938–1962) Lightweight, medium duty integrally built 6-ton F/C 4 w. with Perkins diesel 1939–1956.

1950 JNSN lightweight diesel 6-tonner.

1946 Morris-Commercial 'Equi-Load' forward control 5-tonner.

1951 Shelvoke & Drewry W type 'Freighter'.

SCAMMELL Watford, Herts (1922–1988) Light & medium duty 3 & 4w. tractors; heavy duty N/C 8w. diesel artics & F/C 8w. diesel rigids. Acquired by Leyland in 1955. Became Leyland's Special Products Division in 1972.

S.D. (Shelvoke & Drewry) Letchworth, Herts (1923–1984). (Shelvoke Dempster 1984 to date). Light & medium duty 4 w. F/C petrol and diesel. Mainly specialist chassis for municipal use.

SEDDON Oldham, Lancs (1938–1975) Light, medium & heavy duty 4w N/C & F/C; heavy duty 6 & 8 w. F/C diesel. Took over Atkinson Lorries in 1970. Was taken over itself by International Harvester in 1974. Became Seddon-Atkinson 1975.

SENTINEL Shrewsbury, Salop (1906–1957) Heavy duty 4 & 6 w. F/C diesel. Famous for steam vehicles until 1950. Vehicle interests sold to TVW (North Cheshire Motors) 1957.

KARRIER Huddersfield (1907–1935), Luton, Beds (1935–1976). Light & medium duty 4 w. N/C & F/C petrol and diesel. Specialised in municipal applications. Part of Rootes Group from 1934. Acquired by Chrysler along with Commer in 1973.

LEYLAND Leyland, Lancs (1897–to date) Light and medium 4 w. N/C & F/C petrol and diesel & heavy duty 4, 6 & 8 w. F/C diesel. Leyland absorbed most major UK manufacturers including Albion, AEC, Maudslay, Thornycroft, Guy and Scammell. Leyland was itself merged with DAF in 1987. Products now Leyland-DAF.

MACK Barking, Essex (1954–1964) Medium & heavy duty 4 & 6 w. N/C & F/C diesels. British division of Mack Trucks in USA.

MAUDSLAY Coventry & Alcester, Warwicks. (1904–1958). Heavy duty 4, 6 & 8 w. F/C diesels. Merged into ACV group in 1948. Built Maudslay-badged AECs from 1950.

MORRIS-COMMERCIAL Birmingham (1924–1954). Light & medium duty 4 w. N/C & F/C petrol and diesel. Merged with Austin 1952 to form British Motor Corporation. BMC products named BMC, Austin and Morris from 1956 to 1968. BMC merged with Leyland 1968.

MTN – see 'Rutland'

PAGEFIELD – see.'Walker'

1947 Thornycroft PF/NR6 15-ton 8-wheeler.

1950 Proctor Mark I.

PROCTOR (Proctor Springwood), Mousehold, Norwich (1947–1949). Hereford (1949–1952) Medium duty 4 w. F/C diesel. Manufacture moved to Praills of Hereford in 1949. In 1952 Oswald Tillotson purchased business and production was terminated.

ROWE HILLMASTER Liskeard, Cornwall (1953–1962). Medium & heavy duty 4 & 6 w. F/C diesel.

RUTLAND (Motor Traction Ltd), Croydon, Surrey (1951–58). Medium & heavy duty 4 & 6 w. N/C & F/C diesel. Also listed a rigid 8 w. F/C diesel. Rutlands were also marketed as "M.T.N." and "Manton" in overseas territories.

THORNYCROFT Basingstoke, Hants (1896–1977). Light, medium & heavy duty 4-w. F/C petrol and diesel; heavy duty 6 & 8 w. F/C diesel. Joined ACV Group 1961.

1958 TVW G68 16-ton 8-wheeler.

TVW Warrington, Lancs (1958–1962). Heavy duty 4, 6 & 8 w. F/C diesel. Based on Sentinels but had vertical front mounted engines.

VULCAN Southport, Lancs (1914–1938) Maidstone, Kent (1938–1953). Medium duty 4 w. F/C petrol and diesel. Purchased by Tilling Stevens 1937. Tilling Stevens taken over by Rootes Group in 1950.

WALKER. Wigan, Lancs (1947–1955). Formerly manufacturers of PAGEFIELD (1907–1955) Specialised municipal F/C diesel 4 wheelers.

1954 Rutland 'Return Master' 6-tonner.

INDEX OF ILLUSTRATIONS

ACKNOWLEDGEMENTS

The author gratefully acknowledges the assistance given to him by the .following: Gordon Baron, Malcolm Bates, Derek Bonfield, H.G.Pentus-Brown, Taff Davies, John Douglas, Ieuan Evans, Chris Gardner, Arthur Ingram, Derek Itsinger, Ifan Jones, Roger Kenny, Neil Matlock, Ted Oates, Harry Pick, Bob Rust, Pete Smith, Dave Stewart, Trevor Stone, Ian Trout, Tom Ward, Bert Winkfield, Rick Woodvine.

Grateful thanks also to the many manufacturers, dealers, hauliers, drivers and fellow enthusiasts who have, over the years, supplied the author with information.

Full ahead! An AEC MkIII 8-wheeler 'clogs it' past a slower lorry on the A5 trunk road.